Realities of Faith

by

Umm Muḥammad

King Fahd National Library Cataloging-in-Publication Data

Umm Muhammad
Realities of Faith
96 p, 13.5 X 21 cm.
ISBN 9960-792-13-7
1 - Faith (Islamic creeds) 2 - Islam I - Title

241 dc 0760/15

Legal Deposit no. 0760/15
ISBN: 9960-792-13-7

ABUL-QASIM PUBLISHING HOUSE
Telephone (966) 2 671-4793 – Fax (966) 2 672-5523
P.O. Box 6156
Jeddah 21442, Saudi Arabia

Printed and bound in Saudi Arabia at
Adhwaa AL Bayan Printing Press

Tel: 2434896

THIS BOOK HAS BEEN PRODUCED IN COLLABORATION WITH
ṢAḤEEḤ INTERNATIONAL
Professional Editing and Typesetting of Islamic Literature

TABLE OF CONTENTS

FOREWORD

﴿تَبَارَكَ الَّذِي بِيَدِهِ الـمُلكُ وَهُوَ عَلَى كُلِّ شَيْءٍ قَدِيرٌ الَّذِي خَلَـقَ الـمَوتَ وَالحَيَاةَ لِيَبلُوَكُم أَيُّكُم أَحسَنُ عَمَلاً وَهُوَ العَزِيزُ الغَفُورُ﴾

"Blessed is He in whose hand is Dominion, and He has power over all things – the One who has created death and life to test you [as to] which of you is best in deeds." [1]

* * * * * * *

Realities of faith have always been reflected in human excellence. Indeed Prophet Muḥammad (ﷺ) stated, "I have been sent to perfect the noble traits of character."[2] There is no shortage of proofs in the Qur'ān and the *sunnah* of the fact that morality (both public and private) is an integral part of faith and worship and will be a deciding factor in determining any individual's destiny in the Hereafter.

Yet how often we are confronted with the false and unattractive picture of Islām presented by many Muslims – even some who appear to practice the religion outwardly but are disappointing personalities to those who come in closer contact with them. The unfortunate departure of the masses from Islāmic teachings today is not limited to behavior and conduct alone. If that were so, its treatment would be relatively simple. As a noted author[3] points out, the real problem among contemporary Muslims is none less than a faulty understanding of Islām itself – in particular, the concepts

---

[1] *Sūrah al-Mulk,* 67:1-2.
[2] Al-Bukhārī.
[3] Muḥammad Quṭb in his book *Mafāheem Yanbaghi an Tuṣaḥḥaḥ.*

of *tawḥeed*[4] and worship. Various aspects of these concepts will be treated within the contents of this book, its conclusion being a definitive summary.

The following pages contain a few brief studies pertaining to the heart and soul. They are addressed to believers, and within them are some stops along the path of life which ultimately leads back to the Creator. The subject matter has been taken largely from the writings of early scholars, who, in their own times, were disturbed by changes taking place – not only in society as a whole, but initially in the individual Muslim and his relationship with Allāh. For it is that relationship which must always be the primary concern of the believer, who is mercifully never held accountable for more than his own capacity. Moreover, it is only through the reform of many individual souls that the reform of the community as a whole will follow as a natural result.

The material in this book has been collected by one who is in constant need of such reminders. In sharing it with others, it is hoped that Allāh (*subḥānahu wa ta'ālā*) might accept this small work and in His mercy benefit the writer and reader alike.

﴿إِنَّا عَرَضنَا الأَمَانَةَ عَلَى السَّمَاوَاتِ وَالأَرضِ وَالجِبَالِ فَأَبَينَ أن
يَحمِلنَهَا وَأَشفقنَ مِنهَا وَحَمَلَهَا الإِنسَانُ إِنَّهُ كَانَ ظَلُومًا جَهُولاً﴾

"Verily did We offer the Trust to the heavens and the earth and the mountains, and they refused to bear it and feared it; but man undertook to carry it. Truly was he unjust and ignorant."[5]

The Author
Jeddah, Saudi Arabia
Jumādal-Ākhirah, 1412 / December, 1992

---

[4] Affirming the unity of Allāh and that worship is due to Him alone.
[5] *Sūrah al-Aḥzāb,* 33:72.

AWAKENING

(AT-TANBEEH)

AWAKENING (AT-TANBEEH)

﴿إِنَّ ا للّٰهَ يُمْسِكُ السَّمَاوَاتِ وَالأَرْضَ أَن تَـزُولا. وَلَئِـن زَالَتَـا إِن أَمْسَكَهُمَا مِن أَحَدٍ مِن بَعْدِهِ﴾

"Surely does Allāh hold the heavens and the earth, lest they cease. And if they should cease, none can hold them after Him."[6]

﴿وَمَا خَلَقْنَا السَّمَاوَاتِ وَالأَرْضَ وَمَا بَيْنَهُمَا إِلاَّ بِـالْحَقِّ وَإِنَّ السَّاعَةَ لآتِيَةٌ﴾

"We have not created the heavens and the earth and that between them except in truth, and certainly the Hour is approaching."[7]

﴿وَلَو يُؤَاخِذُ اللّٰهُ النَّاسَ بِمَا كَسَبُوا مَاتَرَكَ عَلَى ظَهْرِهَا مِن دَابَّةٍ وَلَكِن يُؤَخِّرُهُم إِلَى أَجَلٍ مُسَمًّى﴾

"And if Allāh were to impose blame upon the people for what they have earned, He would not leave upon it [i.e., the earth] any creature. But He defers them until an appointed term."[8]

﴿يَاأَيُّهَا الَّذِينَ آمَنُوا اتَّقُوا ا للّٰهَ وَلْتَنظُرْ نَفْسٌ مَا قَدَّمَت لِغَدٍ وَاتَّقُوا ا للّٰهَ﴾

"O you who have believed, fear Allāh. And let every soul look to what it has put forth for tomorrow and fear Allāh."[9]

* * * * * * *

---

[6] *Sūrah Fāṭir,* 35:41.
[7] *Sūrah al-Ḥijr,* 15:85.
[8] *Sūrah Fāṭir,* 35:45.
[9] *Sūrah al-Ḥashr,* 59:18.

All things in creation have a beginning, and our beginning is an awakening... the realization that within oneself all is not well. This awakening may come early in life, or it may come quite late. And even, perhaps, there might be several beginnings after periods of stagnation. Yet, each beginning holds the highest potential, and this is a great mercy from Allāh.

The lifetime is a short journey through one aspect of creation. Its length is not our concern, for Allāh (*subḥānahu wa ta'ālā*) has determined it according to His own knowledge and will, making it entirely adequate for every soul to establish whatever will be a witness for it on the Day of Judgement.

A further mercy to mankind is that every new beginning nullifies all that preceded it, be it disbelief (*kufr*), sin, or mere failure to make the best use of one's time and resources. Prophet Muḥammad (ﷺ) affirmed, "Islām destroys what was before it, and repentance destroys what was before it."[10] What greater generosity could there be than that of Allāh (*subḥānahu wa ta'ālā*), who, after mentioning the eternal humiliation and punishment of those who commit the gravest sins, adds:

﴿إِلَّا مَن تَابَ وَآمَنَ وَعَمِلَ عَمَلًا صَالِحًا فَأُولَٰئِكَ يُبَدِّلُ اللَّهُ سَيِّئَاتِهِمْ حَسَنَاتٍ وَكَانَ اللَّهُ غَفُورًا رَحِيمًا﴾

"...except for those who repent, believe and do good deeds. For them does Allāh convert their evil deeds into good. And Allāh is eternally forgiving and merciful."[11]

Know then, that however long or short a life span might be, its quality, by the grace of Allāh, is determined from that point when one asserts his human faculties of thought and reason and awakens to the purpose of his creation, undertaking

---

[10] Muslim and Aḥmad.
[11] *Sūrah al-Furqān,* 25:70.

to fulfill his responsibilities on earth in obedience to his Creator. The length of this period is again determined by Allāh in adequate measure, according to His perfect knowledge of every soul. From this beginning, true life emerges – life of a higher quality which only the believer can achieve...

﴿أَوَمَن كَانَ مَيتًا فَأَحيَينَاهُ وَجَعَلنَا لَهُ نُورًا يَمشِي بِهِ فِي النَّاسِ
كَمَن مَثَلُهُ فِي الظُّلُمَاتِ لَيسَ بِخَارِجٍ مِنهَا﴾

"And is one who was dead [and] then We gave him life and made for him light by which to walk among the people like one who remains in darkness, never to emerge therefrom?" [12]

The initial awakening in which one chooses Islām over other ways of life is a transition from unawareness to comprehension, from denial to acceptance, from doubt to belief, or from *shirk*[13] to *tawḥeed.*[14] But for the Muslim believer, there is also an awakening – one that leads him from sin to repentance, from various forms of hypocrisy to sincerity, from neglect to responsibility, or from self-satisfaction to higher aspiration. Often it comes gradually as an uneasy feeling – a discomfort of the soul. Then this uneasiness develops into apprehension and finally into the awareness that one is certainly not prepared for death. Facing an undeniable truth, the servant realizes that no excuse will suffice on the Day of Judgement. Through neglect and worldly distractions, he has placed his soul in danger. Frightened by the thought of punishment, he is at once moved to long and strive for that special mercy reserved for those who have earned the acceptance of their Creator in the greater life to come. But in his present state,

---

[12] ***Sūrah al-An'ām,*** 6:122.
[13] The worship of or obedience to others besides Allāh.
[14] Again, there can be no Islām without *tawḥeed.*

would he be accepted? Those diseases of the heart[15] so carefully concealed from his fellow men will certainly be uncovered on that Day... unless they are truly cured. A wise and prudent servant will therefore hasten to grasp the opportunity in his remaining days or hours – an extension granted to him out of mercy from Allāh. For when these have expired, there will be no further respite or chance for amendment...

﴿أَلَمْ يَأْنِ لِلَّذِينَ آمَنُوا أَن تَخْشَعَ قُلُوبُهُمْ لِذِكْرِ اللهِ وَمَا نَزَلَ مِنَ الْحَقِّ وَلَايَكُونُوا كَالَّذِينَ أُوتُوا الْكِتَابَ مِن قَبْلُ فَطَالَ عَلَيْهِمُ الْأَمَدُ فَقَسَتْ قُلُوبُهُمْ وَكَثِيرٌ مِنْهُمْ فَاسِقُونَ﴾

"Has the time not come for those who have believed that their hearts should become humbly submissive at the remembrance of Allāh and what has been revealed of the truth? And [let them] not be like those who were given the Scripture before – then a long period passed over them, and their hearts hardened. And many of them are transgressors." [16]

---

[15]The sinful attitudes and intentions known only to Allāh were referred to by early scholars as "diseases" and are indeed more dangerous than physical illnesses.

[16]*Sūrah al-Ḥadeed*, 57:16. If the *āyah* seems to address today's Muslims, in particular, one might be surprised at the statement of the *ṣaḥābi*, Ibn Mas'ūd: "There was from the time of our accepting Islām until Allāh admonished us in this *āyah* only four years." Such was the concern of Allāh (*subḥānahu wa ta'ālā*) for the Muslim community that He warned even the pious *ṣaḥābah* against deviation and neglect.

TAKING ACCOUNT OF THE SELF

(AL-MUḤĀSABAH)

TAKING ACCOUNT OF THE SELF (AL-MUḤĀSABAH)

﴿الم. أَحَسِبَ النَّاسُ أَن يُترَكُوا أَن يَقُولُوا آمَنَّا وَهُم لايُفتَنُونَ. وَلَقَد فَتَنَّا الَّذِينَ مِن قَبلِهِم فَلَيَعلَمَنَّ اللهُ الَّذِينَ صَدَقُوا وَلَيَعلَمَنَّ الكَاذِبِينَ﴾

"Alif Lām Meem. Do the people think that they will be left to say, 'We believe' and they will not be tried? But We have certainly tested those before them, and indeed, Allāh knows those who are truthful, and He knows those who lie." [17]

* * * * * * *

The duty of enjoining what is right and forbidding what is wrong is especially difficult when practiced on one's own self. Familiarity takes the edge off of criticism; and Shayṭān is ever prepared to defend the erring soul with countless excuses, for this is his last stronghold, and he will never abandon it willingly. When Shayṭān loses hope of affecting a believer's deeds or speech, he seeks to invade the heart and strike at the root of righteousness – intention. By corrupting the intention, he will win the soul; by injecting it with *shirk,* he will make it unacceptable to Allāh (*subḥānahu wa ta'ālā*), because in His sight, "Deeds are only according to intentions."[18] A sensitive believer who knows the weaknesses of the soul can be on guard against the whisperings of Shayṭān and not lose sight of *"aṣ-ṣirāṭ al-mustaqeem."*

'Umar bin al-Khaṭṭāb advised, "Call yourselves to account before you are called to account."; and undoubtedly, Allāh (*subḥānahu wa ta'ālā*) has given us the means by which to do this:

---

[17] ***Sūrah al-'Ankabūt,*** 29:1-3.

[18] Part of a *ḥadīth* narrated by al-Bukhārī and Muslim.

﴿وَهَدَيْنَاهُ النَّجْدَيْنِ﴾

"And We have shown him the two ways."[19]

In other words, mankind has been given the tools with which to distinguish good from evil, and right from wrong: observation, perception, conscience, judgement and emotion, all in a delicate balance. But even so, as we are reminded by Imām Ibn al-Qayyim, such assessment is difficult unless one has the following:

1. The light of wisdom – the light by which Allāh has enlightened the hearts of those who follow the teachings of the prophets
2. The ability to discern between blessings and trials in what Allāh has provided, i.e., one's wealth, time, skills, opportunities, influence, etc. – That which is used in ways pleasing to Allāh contains blessings and benefit, but that which is used otherwise will be evidence against the soul on the Day of Judgement.
3. Suspicion of the self, which leads to a more complete inspection – For indeed, none will harbor a negative thought about his own soul except one who knows it well, while one who thinks well of his soul is most ignorant of himself.[20]

Except for the most private forms of worship, most of our deeds are observed by others and judged by them. However, Allāh (*subḥānahu wa ta'ālā*) is concerned with what is in the heart. "Allāh does not look to your bodies or your faces, but He looks to your hearts and deeds."[21] The quantity of deeds is therefore less important than the quality (how and why). No matter what the impression of our fellow men, the true intention behind every word and action is known only by Allāh,

---

[19]*Sūrah al-Balad,* 90:10.
[20]Words of Ibn al-Qayyim in *Madārij as-Sālikeen.*
[21]Muslim.

and it is He who judges from the position of absolute familiarity with every soul and every circumstance.

﴿يَعْلَمُ خَائِنَةَ الأَعْيُنِ وَمَا تُخْفِي الصُّدُورُ﴾

"He knows that which deceives the eyes and what the breasts conceal." [22]

How easy it is to make excuses or justify oneself to others. However, one must constantly remember that Allāh is aware of the entire truth; therefore, we ourselves must face the truth as well. Speaking directly to His servants in the Qur'ān, Allāh says:

﴿وَاعْلَمُوا أَنَّ اللهَ يَعْلَمُ مَا فِي أَنفُسِكُمْ فَاحْذَرُوهُ﴾

"And know that Allāh knows what is within yourselves; so beware of Him." [23]

﴿وَاعْلَمُوا أَنَّ اللهَ يَحُولُ بَيْنَ الْمَرْءِ وَقَلْبِهِ وَأَنَّهُ إِلَيْهِ تُحْشَرُونَ﴾

"And know that Allāh comes between a man and his heart and that to Him you shall be gathered." [24]

﴿فَإِنَّهُ يَعْلَمُ السِّرَّ وَأَخْفَى﴾

"Truly, He knows the secret and what is [even] more hidden." [25]

﴿فَلَا تُزَكُّوا أَنفُسَكُمْ هُوَ أَعْلَمُ بِمَنِ اتَّقَى﴾

"So do not represent yourselves as righteous, for He knows best who fears Him." [26]

---

[22] *Sūrah Ghāfir*, 40:19.

[23] *Sūrah al-Baqarah*, 2:235.

[24] *Sūrah al-Anfāl*, 8:24.

[25] *Sūrah Ṭā Hā*, 20:7. More hidden than the secret are man's innermost thoughts and intentions.

[26] *Sūrah an-Najm*, 53:32.

﴿وَإِن تُبْدُوا مَا فِي أَنفُسِكُمْ أَوْ تُخْفُوهُ يُحَاسِبْكُم بِهِ اللَّهُ﴾

"Whether you show what is within yourselves or conceal it, Allāh will hold you to account for it."[27]

These verses were terrifying to the Prophet's companions. Because of their intense devotion and their consciousness of Allāh, they often worried about certain thoughts and feelings that came to them, repeatedly asking the Prophet (ﷺ) about them until they were finally reassured, "Allāh has overlooked for me in my community that which occurs to their minds as long as they neither speak of it nor act upon it."[28] The pious companions and their followers were the most critical of their own souls, always seeking to correct themselves in anticipation of the Judgement; and indeed, they were the best of the community. After the Prophet (ﷺ) had confided to Hudhayfah the names of some of the hypocrites, 'Umar asked him fearfully, "Am I among them?" Thus, when Allāh wishes good for His servant, He makes him aware of his own faults.

Keeping the soul in line involves a continuous struggle against Shayṭān:

﴿إِنَّ الشَّيْطَانَ لَكُمْ عَدُوٌّ فَاتَّخِذُوهُ عَدُوًّا﴾

"Certainly, Shayṭān is an enemy to you. So take him as an enemy."[29]

Through knowledge, one can protect himself from Shayṭān, so every believer should be aware of the following facts:

1. Every soul has certain weaknesses, and Shayṭān is always looking for the opportunity to take advantage of them and exploit them to the utmost degree. Each individual soul is susceptible to certain kinds of

---

27 *Sūrah al-Baqarah,* 2:284.

28 Al-Bukhārī, Muslim, at-Tirmidhī, Abū Dāwūd, an-Nasā'ī and Ibn Mājah.

29 *Sūrah Fāṭir,* 35:6.

temptations more than others; thus there is a need for one to recognize his own particular weaknesses and guard against them. In several verses the Qur'ān refers to disbelief (*kufr*) and hypocrisy (*nifāq*) as "disease in the heart." Lesser faults and weaknesses were also labeled by scholars as "diseases of the heart." These include tendencies toward anger, hate, envy, selfishness, conceit or injustice, as well as love of wealth, prestige, physical pleasures or excess – even in those things normally permissible. All of them are doors open to Shayṭān.

2. Two conditions are required for Allāh's acceptance of any deed:
   A. Sincerity of intention, i.e., it must be done for Him alone to seek His pleasure or to prevent His anger – Even ordinary daily tasks become forms of worship when performed with this in mind. Honesty, precision and conscientiousness in every deed is required by Allāh and rewarded by Him.
   B. Correctness – It must be done according to His ordained religion, i.e., lawful according to the Qur'ān and the *sunnah* of the Prophet (ﷺ).

It must be remembered that any action carried out according to erroneous traditions, unlawful innovations or personal preferences can be faulted in both categories. In reference to this, the Qur'ān states:

﴿فَمَن كَانَ يَرجُوا لِقَاءَ رَبِّهِ فَلْيَعمَل عَمَلاً صَالِحًا وَلَا يُشرِك بِعِبَادَةِ رَبِّهِ أَحَدًا﴾

"So whoever hopes to meet his Lord, let him do righteous work and not associate in the worship of his Lord anyone."[30]

---

[30] *Sūrah al-Kahf,* 18:110.

3. *Shirk*[31] destroys any good deeds a person may have done, no matter how great or numerous. And this also is affirmed clearly:

﴿لَئِنْ أَشْرَكْتَ لَيَحْبَطَنَّ عَمَلُكَ﴾

"If you should associate [others with Allāh], your work would perish."[32]

A lesser form of *shirk* is showing one's deeds to others or speaking about them in order to gain respect or some other worldly benefit. This kind of "showing off" is called hidden *shirk* because it is not usually evident to others. In fact, the Prophet (ﷺ) described it as "more hidden than the creeping of ants."[33] Only the sincere believer recognizes hidden *shirk* and feels pain and sadness if he should succumb to it from time to time; but others practice it continually, without even being aware of it. They are the ones who have forgotten Allāh (*subḥānahu wa ta'ālā*) to such an extent that the opinions of people become all-important.

Showing off, when done consciously and purposely, nullifies the deed and can lead to punishment. The Prophet (ﷺ) has stated that the first to be condemned on the Day of Judgement will be a martyr, a *qāri'* (a reciter of the Qur'ān) and a giver of charity. When each of them comes before his Lord declaring that his great work was done for Him, he will be told, "You have lied." Allāh will say to the martyr, "You fought to be called brave, and it was said." And He will say to the reciter, "You learned and taught to be called a scholar, and you recited to be called a *qāri'*; and it was said." And to the charitable one, "You spent to be called generous, and it was said." Then it will be commanded that each be dragged on his

---

[31]Directing worship in the form of good works to other than Allāh, or association by intention.

[32]*Sūrah az-Zumar,* 39:65.

[33]Aḥmad and al-Ḥākim – *ṣaḥeeḥ.*

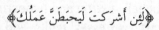

face and thrown into the Fire.[34] Thus, when a person seeks a worldly result, preferring it to the reward of Allāh (*subḥānahu wa ta'ālā*), he can no longer expect that reward in the Hereafter. In another *ḥadīth* it is related: "If someone makes himself heard, Allāh will make heard [that which he concealed]; and if someone shows off, Allāh will expose him."[35] This indicates that those who make their deeds known with the intention of being recognized in this world will be exposed by Allāh on the Day of Judgement when they are most in need of His acceptance.

The following are some examples of deliberate hidden *shirk*:

- Lengthening the prayer, or perhaps, only the period of prostration in the presence of others
- Purposely displaying the effects of fasting, *jihād* or other deeds on the body
- Wearing certain clothing known to be that of ascetics or scholars, or taking care to be seen with them
- Speaking unnecessarily about good deeds done previously, seeking admiration
- Lowering the voice to imply fear of Allāh or other affected mannerisms
- Showing off knowledge or skill in conversation or using the remembrance of Allāh repeatedly to give an impression of piety, or giving advice and warnings in order to be considered a wise and caring benefactor – This is most prevalent among some scholars and religious leaders who feel compelled to live up to the expectations of their followers.

Undoubtedly, there are those who reason that if a deed is done initially with the intention of reward in the Hereafter, then

---

[34] Abridged from a *ḥadīth* narrated by Muslim, at-Tirmidhī and an-Nasā'ī.
[35] Al-Bukhārī, Muslim and others.

what harm is there in looking for a worldly benefit in it as well? But Allāh (*subḥānahu wa ta'ālā*) has disclosed in a *ḥadīth qudsī,* "I am the most self-sufficient of partners, needing no partnership; so if one does a deed for Me and for another [simultaneously], then I am disassociated from it, and it is [only] for the [other] partner."[36]

There are, as well, some non-deliberate mistakes which may lesson one's reward without canceling it completely. These include the following:

- Mentioning one's good works after their completion
- Taking pride inwardly in one's deeds or even in one's sincerity
- Performing righteous works because of pleasure found in them (other than the pleasure of serving Allāh)
- Showing that which reveals much worship on the body or in the voice (other than speech)
- Being unhappy if one's charity or help is not appreciated by the recipient – Appreciation and reward should be expected only from Allāh.
- Finding acts of worship easier to perform if others are aware of them and experiencing pleasure in others' observance of these acts

Those most faithful to Allāh are in constant fear of hidden *shirk,* and they continually exert efforts to conceal their righteous deeds, unless, for some reason, there is more benefit in disclosing them.

At this point, some reassurance may be necessary; for there are things which one might imagine to be *shirk* but are not:

- Accepting thanks or praise for some good which one has done – The Prophet (ﷺ) said, "That is an immediate sign of good tidings for the believer."[37] It is merely a

---

[36]Muslim and Ibn Mājah. A *ḥadīth qudsī* (a *sacred ḥadīth*) is a revelation from Allāh recounted in the words of the Prophet (ﷺ).

[37]Muslim.

preview of what awaits him in the Hereafter, but on the condition that it subsequently does not go to his head. There is no harm in fame gained by a person who does not seek it, but he must take care that it does not corrupt his soul.

- Accepting payment for a job done initially seeking reward from Allāh – Such is the case of one who chooses a certain vocation for which there is a need in the community while he could just as well earn his living in some other way.
- Wearing good clothes – This is not blameworthy unless it is done in conceit, for the purpose of showing off or involves extravagance and waste. As stated in a *ḥadīth*: "When Allāh blesses His servant with a blessing, He likes to see it upon him."[38]
- Setting a good example for others (as a means of teaching)

One should remember the following two points as well:

- Concealing one's sin is a duty. A Muslim should not speak of sins he has committed; rather, he should repent privately and correct his behavior. Then Allāh will conceal that sin for him on the Day of Judgement and forgive him.
- Increasing the amount of worship when one is among a group of worshippers is not considered to be showing off. Because the normal wish of a believer is to worship Allāh, being with a group helps him to overcome certain obstacles (such as his own forgetfulness or laziness) and to realize his original aim.

In an effort to re-institute the true worship of Allāh, scholars have recommended treatments for "diseases of the heart." The foremost of these is the remembrance of Allāh.

---

38 Aṭ-Ṭabarānī – *ṣaḥeeḥ*.

- Remember the greatness of Allāh and then the insignificance of the world and its impermanent state. Remember that the ultimate source of all benefit and harm to yourself and all beings is Allāh. If you fear blame, fear the blame of Allāh; and if you seek praise, hope for the praise of Allāh. Remember that Allāh looks into your heart. Imagine your state if you should die while committing a sin, either openly or secretly – just imagine the humiliation of exposure before all creation on the Day of Judgement. Remember the certainty of death and the shortness of life. Remember the punishment of the grave and that of the Hellfire. Hope for the blessings of Paradise and the pleasure of Allāh.
- Once you are aware of your mistake, turn to Allāh in earnest repentance, asking forgiveness and correcting yourself thereafter. Always be on guard and ask Allāh to help you to avoid falling into such errors in the future. The Prophet (ﷺ) taught his companions this supplication:

  اللّهُمَّ إنّا نَعُوذُ بكَ مِن أن نُشرِكَ بكَ شَيئًا نعلَمُهُ وَنَستغفِرُكَ لِمَا لا نعلَمُه

  "O Allāh, we seek refuge in You from associating with You anything we know of, and we ask Your forgiveness for that which we do not know."[39]
- Make a conscious effort to do more righteous deeds secretly without mentioning them until it becomes a habit.
- Take as friends and companions those you consider to be sincere, righteous and God-fearing. Encourage them to point out your faults and help you to overcome them. Accept advice without anger and try to follow that which is conducive to improvement.
- Finally, do not let Shayṭān prevent your good works by suggesting that you are showing off. If you find

---

[39] Aḥmad.

something of that within yourself, continue your work but correct your intention, seeking acceptance from Allāh alone. For in Allāh's acceptance is salvation and success...

﴿رَبَّنَا لاتُزِغْ قُلُوبَنَا بَعْدَ إِذْ هَدَيْتَنَا وَهَبْ لَنَا مِن لَدُنكَ رَحْمَةً إِنَّكَ أَنتَ الوَهَّابُ﴾

"Our Lord, do not let our hearts deviate after You have guided us, and give us from Yourself mercy. Indeed, it is You who is the Giver [of all things]." [40]

---

40 *Sūrah Āli 'Imrān,* 3:8.

REPENTANCE

(AT-TAWBAH)

REPENTANCE (AT-TAWBAH)

Allāh (*subḥānahu wa ta'ālā*) orders all believers to repent:

﴿وَتُوبُوا إِلَى اللهِ جَمِيعًا أَيُّهَا الْمُؤْمِنُونَ لَعَلَّكُمْ تُفْلِحُونَ﴾

"And turn all of you in repentance to Allāh, O believers, that you may succeed." [41]

﴿يَاأَيُّهَا الَّذِينَ آمَنُوا تُوبُوا إِلَى اللهِ تَوْبَةً نَصُوحًا﴾

"O you who have believed, repent to Allāh with sincere repentance." [42]

And He warns:

﴿وَمَن لَم يَتُب فَأُولَئِكَ هُمُ الظَّالِمُونَ﴾

"And whoever does not repent – those are the unjust." [43]

And He affirms:

﴿إِنَّ اللهَ يُحِبُّ التَّوَّابِينَ وَيُحِبُّ الْمُتَطَهِّرِينَ﴾

"Indeed, Allāh loves those who repent, and He loves those who purify themselves." [44]

Repentance is required for all sins, great or small, apparent or hidden. It is for the benefit of man, since Allāh Himself is free of need.

The word *"tawbah"* (repentance) literally means "turning back." Since sin puts distance between the soul and Allāh (*subḥānahu wa ta'ālā*), during repentance the servant turns back to Allāh, seeking refuge in His forgiveness. And when a

---

41 *Sūrah an-Nūr,* 24:31.
42 *Sūrah at-Taḥreem,* 66:8.
43 *Sūrah al-Ḥujurāt,* 49:11.
44 *Sūrah al-Baqarah,* 2:222.

soul repents and returns to Him, Allāh turns back to His servant in acceptance and forgiveness. Thus Allāh has named Himself "*at-Tawwāb*" (the Constant Acceptor of Repentance), sometimes translated as "the Oft-Returning."

Since man is created in weakness and imperfection, error is part of his nature. But all sinners are not the same. They generally fall into two categories: those who follow the path of Shayṭān (who refused obedience and repentance out of conceit) and are thus doomed to the Hellfire, and those who have been promised forgiveness and Paradise:

﴿وَالَّذِينَ إِذَا فَعَلُوا فَاحِشَةً أَوْ ظَلَمُوا أَنفُسَهُمْ ذَكَرُوا اللَّهَ فَاسْتَغْفَرُوا لِذُنُوبِهِمْ وَمَن يَغْفِرُ الذُّنُوبَ إِلَّا اللَّهُ﴾

> ***"...those who, when they commit an immorality or wrong themselves [by transgression], remember Allāh and seek forgiveness for their sins. And who can forgive sins except Allāh?"*** [45]

A prerequisite to repentance is the knowledge and admission of sin, for ignorance and denial are barriers, preventing return. Knowledge of the consequences of sin, both in this world and in the next, will make one most anxious to escape the result of his carelessness. And where can he find refuge and protection from that except with Allāh (*subḥānahu wa ta'ālā*)? Therefore, one should consider the reason he fell into sin, which is that he, at least temporarily, forgot Allāh. And when a servant forgets Him and drifts away, Allāh removes His protection from that soul, leaving him to depend only upon himself. Thus he becomes prey to his own desires and to Shayṭān. If he had remembered his Lord at the time of temptation, he would have retained Allāh's protection from sin. Indeed, every moment of his life, man is in one of two states:

---

[45] *Sūrah Āli 'Imrān,* 3:135.

either that of remembrance, holding fast to Allāh and thereby placing his soul under His custody, or that of forgetfulness, breaking away from the protective custody of Allāh.

A temporary slip into some form of sin is usually checked by the believer before too long. No sooner has he committed the sin than he feels pain. Even the pleasure expected from that sin which initially tempted him eludes him, and he finds in his heart only sadness at the realization that Allāh has left him to himself.

Certain souls, however, find pleasure in disobedience. They are like those people who, although harboring a fatal illness, refuse to admit it or to seek treatment. The amount of pleasure reflects: 1) the extent of one's desire for the unlawful, 2) his ignorance concerning Him whom he has disobeyed and 3) his ignorance of the Hereafter. One's happiness with the unlawful is indeed more harmful to him than the sin itself, for it shows a conscience which is lifeless and devoid of function. When unawareness has reached such a degree that it finally becomes persistence in sin and insistence upon it, Allāh's punishment is swift. He allows that soul to fall even deeper into sin until it reaches the state described in the Qur'ān:

﴿كَلاَّ بَلْ رَانَ عَلَى قُلُوبِهِم مَا كَانُوا يَكْسِبُونَ﴾

> ***"No, but stain has covered their hearts from that which they have earned."***[46]

Concerning this, the Prophet (ﷺ) explained, "When the servant commits a sin, a black mark is etched onto his heart, but if he ceases and asks Allāh's forgiveness, then his heart is wiped clean. If, however, he repeats it, then it [i.e., the black stain] increases until it eventually envelops the heart. This is the stain which Allāh has mentioned in His Book."[47] Qur'ānic commentators describe the stain as sin upon sin, which finally

---

[46] *Sūrah al-Muṭaffifeen,* 83:14.

[47] Aḥmad, at-Tirmidhī and an-Nasā'ī – *ḥasan.*

blackens the heart until no light of truth can penetrate into it and until the soul subsequently rejects truth and guidance altogether. The greatest sins, however, are those done publicly. It is then that the offending soul is either in open rebellion against Allāh or complete disbelief.

Yet, repentance is always possible. Allāh provides us with hope:

﴿قُل يَا عِبَادِيَ الَّذِينَ أَسْرَفُوا عَلَى أَنْفُسِهِم لَا تَقْنَطُوا مِن رَّحْمَةِ اللَّهِ إِنَّ اللَّهَ يَغْفِرُ الذُّنُوبَ جَمِيعًا إِنَّهُ هُوَ الْغَفُورُ الرَّحِيمُ﴾

"Say, 'O My servants who have committed excess against themselves, do not despair of Allāh's mercy. Indeed, Allāh forgives all sins, for it is He who is the Ever-Forgiving, Merciful.'" [48]

Since repentance is accepted only from a Muslim submitting himself to Allāh, the repentance of a non-believer or one who has committed *shirk* is accomplished by his entry or re-entry into Islām. Moreover, since it is, in fact, a return to Allāh, repentance requires a knowledge of Him and the knowledge that the erring soul has been very distant from Him. Such a soul has been a prisoner of its enemy, Shayṭān, due to its unawareness of Allāh and its own insolence. Thus, it requires an extensive search into how and why that came about and an acceptance of the knowledge that there can be no excuse for disobedience after an order or prohibition is known. [49] It also requires a realization that true repentance is a

---

[48] *Sūrah az-Zumar*, 39:53.

[49] Ibn al-Qayyim points out that one who neglects the right of his Lord, blaming his sin on divine decree to absolve himself of responsibility, has committed an additional offense. Would he himself accept this argument from a disobedient wife or from someone who had cheated him? On the contrary, his anger would be further increased by such an excuse so obviously out of place. Yet, he readily uses the same reasoning against Allāh (*subḥānahu wa taʿālā*), who is far above any injustice. See *Tah-dheeb Madārij as-Sālikeen*, page 127.

difficult task, demanding great effort and consciousness, and that the effort must be in direct proportion to the distance of one's deviation from the Straight Path.

Repentance is subject to certain conditions: regret, cessation, apology and rectification. When all of them are met, the servant is considered to have returned to Allāh and to the state of worship for which he was created.[50] Each condition will be examined briefly:

1. Regret and remorse must replace the acceptance and satisfaction which allow the continuation of a sin. It is pain felt in the heart at a loss for which there is personal responsibility – a loss that could have been prevented. In this case, it refers to the loss of Allāh's protection and the nearness to Him which gives peace of mind. In addition, there is fear following the realization of the seriousness of that offense that has damaged the soul and of the severe penalty of the Hereafter, which can only be avoided through Allāh's mercy. As with the loss of a dear one or of a valuable friendship, pain is evident in prolonged sorrow and weeping. The offender wishes intensely that he had never committed such an error and desperately seeks some means to amend the situation.
2. Cessation is imperative. Repentance is not possible while one is still committing the sin. In fact, persistence in a small sin increases it until it carries the weight of a great sin. The offender must desist immediately, determining not to return to that offense ever again. If, however, through human weakness and in spite of earnest effort one should again fall into the same sin, he must repent again and renew his resolve to avoid that error, for Allāh never refuses sincere repentance.

---

50 Allāh says: ﴿وَمَا خَلَقْتُ الجِنَّ وَالإِنسَ إِلا لِيَعْبُدُونِ﴾ ***"And I did not create jinn and men except to worship Me."*** (*Sūrah adh-Dhāriyāt,* 51:56)

3. Apology to Allāh is in order. Sin acts as a barrier between man and his Lord; therefore, one must seek forgiveness through repeated prayer and supplication, humbly admitting to Allāh his weakness, his need for His mercy and protection, and the gravity of what he has done. Begging Allāh to accept his repentance and to return him to His grace through His generosity, the servant is most acutely aware of his dependence and fallibility. After having been seduced into disobedience by Shayṭān, our father and prophet, Ādam, was taught words of repentance by Allāh:

﴿قَالَا رَبَّنَا ظَلَمْنَا أَنفُسَنَا وَإِن لَّمْ تَغْفِرْ لَنَا وَتَرْحَمْنَا لَنَكُونَنَّ مِنَ الْخَاسِرِينَ﴾

"Our Lord, we have wronged our souls, so if You do not forgive us and have mercy upon us, [then] we will surely be among the losers."[51]

4. Rectification applies both to the relationship between oneself and Allāh (*subḥānahu wa ta'ālā*), which must be amended, and to the rights of one's fellow human beings. Certain acts (such as violations of *iḥrām*, breaking oaths and accidental killing) require a *kaffārah* (expiation); yet, in most cases involving obligations to Allāh alone, the conditions of regret, cessation and apology are the only requirements for forgiveness. However, a person who is especially anxious to regain the pleasure of Allāh (fearing a fault in his repentance) can undertake to do extra deeds of righteousness such as additional prayers, fasting or charity – in short, any lawful means of worship. And always, an excellent

---

[51] *Sūrah al-A'rāf,* 7:23.

deed in the sight of Allāh is one which benefits others in some way. Indeed, such acts are expiation for sins:

﴿إِنَّ الْحَسَنَاتِ يُذْهِبْنَ السَّيِّئَاتِ﴾

"Verily, good deeds do away with bad ones." [52]

As for injury done to another party (which is disobedience to Allāh as well), the damage must be restored or adequately compensated for whenever possible, or the forgiveness of the other party must be obtained.[53] For example, if property has been taken in an unlawful manner or damaged, it must be returned or replaced (even if this might involve a long search for someone wronged years ago, or if he has died, for his heirs). In the case of harm done by word of mouth (as through false witness or slander), one must make the utmost effort to right this wrong by confessing openly and asking forgiveness of the victim. If it is thought that (as in some cases of backbiting and gossip of which the victim is unaware) admission might lead to further problems, one should certainly take care to speak well of that person on future occasions and ask forgiveness from Allāh. Sometimes it is not possible to restore a right completely, due to the enormity of the offense or the inaccessibility of the victim. Therefore, it is incumbent upon the offender to do good deeds which will benefit the injured party or his heirs. If that, too, is impossible, then he can at least continue to make supplication for the injured party, asking Allāh to benefit him (or them) where he himself has failed.

Allāh (*subḥānahu wa ta'ālā*) promises acceptance of true repentance:

---

52 *Sūrah Hūd,* 11:114.

53 Legal punishments for certain crimes serve not only to benefit society but to completely purify a soul which has repented for that sin to Allāh. But for an unrepentant soul (or one who regrets only from fear of worldly punishment), legal retribution will not lessen the extreme punishments of the Hereafter.

﴿كَتَبَ رَبُّكُمْ عَلَىٰ نَفْسِهِ الرَّحْمَةَ أَنَّهُ مَنْ عَمِلَ مِنكُمْ سُوءًا بِجَهَالَةٍ ثُمَّ تَابَ مِن بَعْدِهِ وَأَصْلَحَ فَأَنَّهُ غَفُورٌ رَّحِيمٌ﴾

"Your Lord has decreed upon Himself mercy – that any of you who does a wrong in ignorance,[54] then repents after that and corrects himself, [will be forgiven, for] certainly is He forgiving and merciful."[55]

Yet how easy is repentance of the tongue alone! It would therefore be suspect if sadness is fleeting and quickly forgotten, if pleasure is felt upon remembering the sin, if determination to reform is weak, and if one is immediately satisfied that he has repented and does not increase in righteousness as a result. Repentance is unacceptable if done for any reason other than the fear of Allāh, such as outward appearance, avoidance of blame by others, lack of means to continue the sin, or loss of desire due to contentment, illness or age. In truth, one should beware lest his repentance be defaulted.

Thus genuine repentance is recognized by certain particulars. Among them are the fear of a fault which might prevent its acceptance, extreme caution to avoid anything leading back to that sin or something similar, sadness which brings tears, and remorse which prevents pleasure in any of life's activities. Among them as well are the admission that Allāh has every right to punish the offender severely, a heart gripped by fear and embarrassment before Allāh, and a body burdened under the weight of guilt... And among the signs is the realization that the person is definitely better than he was before the sin was committed!

This is a state which is loved by Allāh – the intense longing of His servant for Him and for His acceptance after he has experienced its loss, the need of the servant to return to Him.

---

54 A believer would not commit wrong deliberately – only through unawareness or forgetfulness.

55 *Sūrah al-An'ām*, 6:54.

The Prophet (ﷺ) once said, "Indeed Allāh is happier with the repentance of His servant than one of you would be if he came across his camel after he had lost it in a wide, open land."[56] And he (ﷺ) affirmed, "Allāh, the Exalted, extends His hand by night for the repentance of he who has sinned by day; and He extends His hand by day for the repentance of he who has sinned by night – until the sun rises from the west."[57]

The immediate fruit of repentance is a lesson learned and a new awareness and sensitivity. The believer's soul is purified by Allāh's forgiveness and acceptance, and his character is improved by the new traits which he has acquired through his experience. His own faults apparent to him, he is not occupied with the faults of others but lives with the words of Allāh:

﴿وَلَوْلَا فَضْلُ اللَّهِ عَلَيْكُمْ وَرَحْمَتُهُ مَا زَكَى مِنكُم مِّنْ أَحَدٍ أَبَدًا وَلَٰكِنَّ اللَّهَ يُزَكِّي مَن يَشَاءُ﴾

"And if not for the favor of Allāh upon you, not one of you would have been pure. But Allāh purifies whom He wills."[58]

Thus the believer is comforted and relieved by the knowledge that, in His mercy, Allāh has made him aware of his sin so that he may repent; and after exerting sincere efforts in repentance and the performance of righteous deeds, he can trust that the past is no longer a barrier between himself and the pleasure of Allāh, who says:

﴿وَإِنِّي لَغَفَّارٌ لِّمَن تَابَ وَآمَنَ وَعَمِلَ صَالِحًا ثُمَّ اهْتَدَىٰ﴾

"Indeed I am the Perpetual Forgiver of whoever repents and believes and does good and then is rightly guided."[59]

---

56 Al-Bukhārī, Muslim and others. Allāh's happiness is because of His grace, as He is free of need.

57 Signaling the imminence of the Day of Judgement. Narrated by Muslim.

58 *Sūrah an-Nūr,* 24:21.

59 *Sūrah Ṭā Hā,* 20:82.

His new relationship with Allāh reflects upon and affects all aspects of his life, and his eagerness to preserve that close tie keeps him constantly on guard.

We must remember that Shayṭān is persistent and slow to give up. If he cannot keep a servant in disbelief, he will make deviation and innovation in religion seem pleasing to him. If he fails in that, then he will try to lead him into a major or a minor sin. If this, too, is futile, then he will seek to occupy one with that which is lawful and permissible in order to keep him from that which is more pleasing to Allāh. And finally, when all else fails, he will content himself with leading the servant to the lesser of two good deeds. Yet, for one alert to them, Shayṭān's strategies can be easily recognized and defeated.

Repentance from sin is a steppingstone to continued righteousness – a return to inner harmony and to Allāh.

﴿إِنَّ اللهَ يُحِبُّ التَّوَّابِينَ وَيُحِبُّ الْمُتَطَهِّرِينَ﴾

"Verily does Allāh love those who constantly repent and those who purify themselves."[60]

Taking account of one's self is consistently required in all things, whether apparent or hidden. While ordinary people might regard certain sins as unimportant, the believer, when acknowledging the right of Allāh over him and his indebtedness to Him, sees them as ugly and dangerous. As a result, he cannot but see his good deeds as insignificant in this light, and therefore, he strives continuously to increase them. The Prophet (ﷺ) taught the best supplication for forgiveness:

اللّٰهُمَّ أنتَ رَبِّي لا إِلٰهَ إلاَّ أنتَ. خَلَقْتَنِي وَأَنَا عَبدُكَ وَأَنَا عَلَى عَهدِكَ وَوَعدِكَ مَا استَطَعتُ. أَعُوذُ بِكَ مِن شَرِّ مَا صَنَعتُ. أَبُوءُ لَكَ بِنِعمَتِكَ عَلَيَّ وَأَبُوءُ بِذَنبِي فَاغفِر لِي فَإِنَّهُ لاَيَغفِرُ الذُّنُوبَ إِلاَّ أَنتَ.

60 *Sūrah al-Baqarah,* 2:222.

"O Allāh, You are my Lord – there is no god but You. You created me, and I am Your servant; and I uphold Your covenant and [my] promise to You as much as I am able. I seek refuge in You from the evil I have done. I acknowledge before You Your favor upon me, and I acknowledge my sin, so forgive me. Indeed, there is none who can forgive sins except You."[61]

Repentance is a new beginning, as illustrated in the saying of the Prophet (ﷺ): "Islām destroys what came before it, and repentance destroys what came before it."[62] Therefore, no soul should ever despair – no matter how great its sin – for Allāh is near, ever-ready to receive repentance, willing to forgive, inviting all to forgiveness with the words:

﴿قُلْ يَاعِبَادِيَ الَّذِينَ أَسْرَفُوا عَلَى أَنفُسِهِمْ لَاتَقْنَطُوا مِن رَحْمَةِ اللهِ إِنَّ اللهَ يَغْفِرُ الذُّنُوبَ جَمِيعًا إِنَّهُ هُوَ الْغَفُورُ الرَّحِيمُ﴾

"Say, 'O My servants who have committed excess [i.e., sinned] against themselves, do not despair of Allāh's mercy. Certainly does Allāh forgive all sins, for it is He who is the Ever-Forgiving, Merciful.' "[63]

---

61 Al-Bukhārī.

62 Al-Bukhārī.

63 *Sūrah az-Zumar,* 39:53.

PATIENCE

(AṢ-ṢABR)

PATIENCE (AṢ-ṢABR)

﴿إِنَّمَا يُوَفَّى الصَّابِرُونَ أَجرَهُم بِغَيرِ حِسَابٍ﴾

"Indeed, those who are patient will be given their reward without enumeration."[64]

* * * * * * *

It has been pointed out that patience is a particular characteristic of human beings; it is not generally found in animals due to the dominance of their instincts, nor is it present in angels, who, by their nature, are free from desire. As for man, he is created in the early stage of life like the animal, with instincts dominant and little ability for patience. Then as his mind awakens and develops understanding, he is guided to the advantage gained by patience in many situations, although this is incomplete guidance and does not go beyond the benefits of worldly life. Then, if he should come to know the guidance of Allāh (*subḥānahu wa ta'ālā*) and what relates to the Hereafter, his motivation for patience is strengthened further. However, his nature still inclines towards what he likes, causing that inner struggle in which patience is described as "the firmness of the religious incentive in the face of an onslaught of passions." This type of resistance is what is particular to believers and is a primary cause for entry into Paradise.

Patience or forbearance has been mentioned in some 90 places in the Qur'ān, and it is considered a duty upon every Muslim by the authority of the Qur'ān, the *sunnah* and the consensus of scholars. Yet it is one of the most difficult forms of worship for man if he has not already accustomed himself to it or practiced it regularly to gain competence. If his nature pulls him towards that which he likes, then patience requires that he experience and accept that which he dislikes. Thus,

---

64 *Sūrah az-Zumar,* 39:10.

compensation in the Hereafter is promised to be far beyond what the servant deserves, continuing on and on with no account being taken of Allāh's unlimited generosity.

The linguistic definition of *ṣabr* is "restraint and confinement" – restraining the soul from panic, anger or greed; restraining the tongue from complaint; and restraining the limbs from improper action. Islāmic scholars have generally divided patience into three categories:

1. Patience to obey Allāh in what He has ordered – Patience in obedience is required since the human soul seeks comfort and ease, is reluctant to give it up, and by nature, dislikes subjection. Laziness and love of possessions must be overcome by patience in such duties as prayer, *zakāh* and *jihād.* When performing any deed for the acceptance of Allāh, one must be patient before beginning it by perfecting the intention and opposing the urge to show off. He must be patient during the deed itself not to forget Allāh and to make the deed as good and complete as possible. And finally, he must be patient afterwards in avoiding pride or expecting gratitude from fellow men.

 ﴿وَاصبِر نَفسَكَ مَعَ الَّذِينَ يَدعُونَ رَبَّهُم بِالغَدَاةِ وَالعَشِيِّ يُرِيدُونَ وَجهَهُ﴾

 "And keep yourself patient with those who call upon their Lord morning and evening, seeking His acceptance."[65]

2. Patience to refrain from disobedience – The Prophet (ﷺ) once said, "The world is the believer's prison and the non-believer's paradise."[66] For those who have been accustomed to living a lifestyle far from the Straight Path, patience is required after repentance in order to

[65] ***Sūrah al-Kahf,*** 18:28.
[66] Muslim.

keep Shayṭān at bay. Indeed, each new temptation must be resisted vigorously. The most difficult in this category is the avoidance of those sins – such as backbiting – which are committed easily and not always deplored by others as well as those sins which are usually committed secretly.

3. Patience in the face of problems or afflictions – This category includes all that happens to one against his own will, such as the loss of property, the death of loved ones, illness, or harm done to him by others – the most difficult of all to bear gracefully! Allāh (*subḥānahu wa ta'ālā*) tells us:

﴿وَلَنَبْلُوَنَّكُم بِشَيْءٍ مِنَ الْخَوفِ وَالْجُوعِ وَنَقْصٍ مِنَ الأَمْوَالِ وَالأَنفُسِ وَالثَّمَرَاتِ وَبَشِّرِ الصَّابِرِينَ الَّذِينَ إِذَا أَصَابَتْهُم مُصِيبَةٌ قَالُوا إِنَّا لِلَّهِ وَإِنَّا إِلَيْهِ رَاجِعُونَ أُولَـٰئِكَ عَلَيْهِمْ صَلَوَاتٌ مِن رَبِّهِمْ وَرَحْمَةٌ وَأُولَـٰئِكَ هُمُ الْمُهْتَدُونَ﴾

"And We shall certainly test you with something of fear and hunger and loss of wealth and lives and fruits, but give glad tidings to the patient, who, when they are struck by disaster, say, 'We belong to Allāh and to Him we will return.' Those are the ones who have upon them blessings from their Lord and mercy. And those are the ones who are guided."[67]

Such trials from Allāh – no matter how distasteful to the servant – are, in reality, opportunities for him. The Prophet (ﷺ) reported, "There is no disaster which befalls the Muslim by which Allāh does not remove sins from him – even [as little as] the thorn that pricks him."[68]

---

67 *Sūrah al-Baqarah,* 2:155-157.
68 Al-Bukhārī and Muslim.

Patience in the face of mishaps and difficulties and acceptance of Allāh's will and wisdom in such matters are proof of faith. This does not mean that dislike of what has occurred is wrong, for feelings of loss, frustration and pain are a normal part of human life.

﴿لَقَدْ خَلَقْنَا الإِنسَانَ فِي كَبَدٍ﴾

"Verily, We have created mankind into hardship."[69]

It is imperative to remember that although feelings will not be judged, reactions will be. In the words of the Prophet (ﷺ): "Allāh will not punish for tears in the eyes nor for sadness in the heart; but He will punish for this [and he pointed to his tongue] or grant mercy."[70] At the death of his son, Ibrāheem, he (ﷺ) said, "The eye weeps and the heart is sad, but we will not say except what pleases our Lord."[71]

Undoubtedly, those whose faith is weak will show it in times of severe trial. Protest against divine decree, anger against Allāh, turning away from Him through neglect of prayer and other duties, or outright denial of Him are all signs of failure in one's examination and damage to his soul.

﴿وَمِنَ النَّاسِ مَن يَعْبُدُ اللهَ عَلَى حَرْفٍ فَإِنْ أَصَابَهُ خَيْرٌ اطْمَأَنَّ بِهِ وَإِنْ أَصَابَتْهُ فِتْنَةٌ انقَلَبَ عَلَى وَجْهِهِ خَسِرَ الدُّنْيَا وَالآخِرَةَ﴾

"And among the people is he who worships Allāh on an edge. If he is touched by good, he is reassured by it; but if he is struck by trial, he turns on his face [to the other direction]. He has lost this world and the Hereafter."[72]

---

69 *Sūrah al-Balad,* 90:4.
70 Al-Bukhārī and Muslim.
71 Al-Bukhārī.
72 *Sūrah al-Ḥajj,* 22:11.

In contrast, when patience *is* practiced, seeking blessing and reward from Allāh, and when the servant is certain of the positive results, it will turn into acceptance, which overcomes bitterness in the soul.

Obviously, it is not fitting that a servant complains to others about Allāh; but, on the contrary, complaints directed to Allāh about certain oppressors or difficult circumstances are an indication of trust in Him. Prophet Ya'qūb said:

﴿قَالَ إِنَّمَا أَشْكُو بَثِّي وَحُزْنِي إِلَى اللَّهِ﴾

> ***"I only complain of my suffering and sadness to Allāh."***[73]

Supplications for help or relief do not indicate impatience, but rather, they are pleasing to Allāh; and at such times response is very near. Additionally, the unlimited reward awaiting those who show forbearance, only seeking refuge in Allāh, is such that it gives the greatest comfort to the believer. In the Qur'ān we are told:

﴿قُل لَّن يُصِيبَنَا إِلَّا مَا كَتَبَ اللَّهُ لَنَا﴾

> ***"Say, 'Never will we be struck except by what Allāh has decreed for us.'"***[74]

Note that He (*subḥānahu wa ta'ālā*) does not use the words "upon us" or "against us." Indeed, affliction is dreaded and disliked because it is most difficult to bear; yet He who loves His servants and cares for them absolutely has chosen to give them opportunities for eternal Paradise. In essence, He has decreed such trials *for us* if only we would reflect.

Not only does a servant obtain additional reward through his afflictions, but upon being disabled either temporarily or permanently, one continues to gain that which he was

---

[73] ***Sūrah Yūsuf,*** 12:86.
[74] ***Sūrah at-Tawbah,*** 9:51.

accustomed to earning through his usual righteous deeds and actions previous to the disability. For the Prophet (ﷺ) informed us that Allāh (*subḥānahu wa ta'ālā*) commands the recording angels, "Register for My servant during every day and night whatever good he used to do for as long as he is confined in My restriction."[75]

A question to be considered at this point is: "What is the manner in which a Muslim should face a situation requiring patience?"

When one admits the unconditional right of Allāh to do as He pleases with His creation, trusting in the ultimate good of His decrees, he will prepare himself continually for the possibility of examination through painful experiences. In fact, this expectation helps him to retain control in the crucial period specified by the Prophet (ﷺ) in the *ḥadīth*: "Patience is [necessary] at the first shock."[76]

In times of trial one should turn to Allāh for consolation and compensation. Umm Salamah reported that she heard the Messenger of Allāh (ﷺ) say, "No servant is struck by affliction and then says, 'We belong to Allāh and to Him we will return. O Allāh, reward me in my affliction and follow it up with something better for me,' without Allāh rewarding him in his affliction and following it with something better for him." She added, "So when Abu Salamah passed away, I said as the Messenger of Allāh had ordered, and Allāh followed that up with what was better for me than him – the Messenger of Allāh [himself]."[77]

One of the Prophet's companions, Sa'd bin Abī Waqqāṣ, once asked, "O Messenger of Allāh, which people are most severely tried?" The Prophet (ﷺ) answered, "The prophets, then the righteous, then those following them in degree. A man is tried according to his religion. So, if there is firmness in

---

75 Al-Ḥākim – *ṣaḥeeḥ*.
76 Al-Bukhārī and Muslim.
77 Aḥmad and Muslim.

his religion, then his trial is increased; but if there is weakness in his religion, then it is lightened. Verily, tribulations remain with the servant until he walks upon the earth having no sin left upon him."[78]

A point worth mentioning is that affliction is not always in the form of sudden disaster. It might be a prolonged state of difficulties such as illness, poverty or oppression by others. Again, believers find aid during such trials by doing the following:

1. Remembering the great reward awaiting those who practice patience and forbearance – Imagine yourself receiving a compensation of such magnitude as to overcome all that you have suffered.
2. Looking forward to relief from the difficulty as well as planning for that time, which lightens the burden of waiting – Trust that you are close to Allāh during this period, that your supplication is being heard and that He will certainly support you.

﴿فَإِنَّ مَعَ الْعُسْرِ يُسْرًا إِنَّ مَعَ الْعُسْرِ يُسْرًا﴾

"For verily, with hardship comes ease. Verily with hardship comes ease."[79]

Do not despair. Know that you have the ability to endure whatever comes your way no matter how heavy the burden seems at the moment because, as He states in the Qur'ān:

﴿لاَ يُكَلِّفُ اللهُ نَفْسًا إِلاَّ وُسْعَهَا﴾

"Allāh charges no soul except [with that which is] within its capacity."[80]

---

78 At-Tirmidhī – *ḥasan ṣaḥeeḥ.*
79 ***Sūrah ash-Sharḥ,*** 94:5-6.
80 ***Sūrah al-Baqarah,*** 2:286.

3. Trusting that however distasteful certain experiences seem to be, there is good in them according to the perfect knowledge of Allāh (*subḥānahu wa ta'ālā*).

﴿وَعَسَى أَن تَكْرَهُوا شَيْئًا وَهُوَ خَيْرٌ لَّكُمْ وَعَسَى أَن تُحِبُّوا شَيْئًا وَهُوَ شَرٌّ لَّكُمْ وَاللَّهُ يَعْلَمُ وَأَنتُمْ لَا تَعْلَمُونَ﴾

"And perhaps you hate something while it is good for you, and perhaps you love something while it is bad for you; and Allāh knows, and you know not."[81]

4. Counting the blessings which Allāh has bestowed – great and small, obvious and subtle – When one finds himself unable to account for all of them, the difficulty is lightened in his eyes. Reward is gained by praising Allāh in every circumstance, especially when realizing that the blessings retained after a loss are still far greater than those of which one was deprived. Indeed, one appreciates his own condition more when comparing it with others whose afflictions are greater than his own. The Prophet (ﷺ) taught that upon seeing the suffering of others, one should say to himself, "Praise be to Allāh, who has exempted me from that by which He has tested you, and who has favored me with preference over many of those whom He has created."[82] He (ﷺ) further advised, "Look to those below you [i.e., those with less than you] and do not look to those above you [i.e., those with more than you], for this makes you less likely to underestimate Allāh's blessings upon you."[83]

---

[81] *Sūrah al-Baqarah,* 2:216.
[82] At-Tirmidhī – *ḥasan.*
[83] Muslim and others.

As well as the aforementioned statements, it is necessary to remember that appreciation of blessings is complementary to patience. Many servants of Allāh are tested through His favors upon them, and this might be, in fact, the most difficult of trials; for one who constantly turns to Allāh while seeking relief in hardship might well forget Him once the crisis has passed and he is once again secure. Additionally, he might also forget that thankfulness is not merely *"al-ḥamdu lillāh"* pronounced by the tongue alone; but rather, it is proven by obedience to Allāh and by sharing one's blessings with those in need. In reality:

﴿وَقَلِيلٌ مِنْ عِبَادِيَ الشَّكُورُ﴾

"Few of My servants are thankful." [84]

One should be aware that in every case of poverty, illness, fear or loss there are points to remember which require gratitude to Allāh:

1. That He (*subḥānahu wa ta'ālā*) prevented the ordeal from being greater than it was
2. That since it was decreed for the servant and therefore inevitable, it has now occurred and is no longer before him
3. That this trial was an expiation for sins, and as such, the penalty was not postponed until the Hereafter, where it would have been much more severe
4. That even in one's own lifetime, certain benefits may be gained from such an experience, for example the strengthening of character or a lesson learned – In any case, the reward is always greater than the adversity.
5. That the casualty was not the servant's religion, i.e., he did not lose his faith or his resolve – Once when a man said to Sahl bin 'Abdullāh, "A thief entered my house

---

84 *Sūrah Saba'*, 34:13.

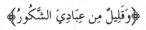

and stole my property," Sahl replied, "If Shayṭān had entered your heart and spoiled your faith, then what would you have done? One who deserved to be beaten one hundred lashes and got off with only ten certainly ought to be thankful!"

There has been much speculation about which is best – patience or thankfulness – but, in reality, there are degrees of each. Patience begins with control, but acceptance is better; and gratitude for recognized blessings is good, but thankfulness during trials of hardship is better. Thus patience and thankfulness merge at the highest level in the soul of the Muslim believer whose hope lies in Allāh and the Last Day. And to Allāh is due all praise and gratitude.

﴿لَئِن شَكَرۡتُمۡ لَأَزِيدَنَّكُمۡ وَلَئِن كَفَرۡتُمۡ إِنَّ عَذَابِي لَشَدِيدٞ﴾

"If you are thankful, then I will increase you [in favor]; but if you deny, certainly My punishment is severe."[85]

---

[85] *Sūrah Ibrāheem,* 14:7.

THE FEELING OF ALIENATION

(AL-GHURBAH)

THE FEELING OF ALIENATION
(AL-GHURBAH)

﴿فَلَا يَغْرُرْكَ تَقَلُّبُهُم فِي البِلَادِ﴾

"...so do not be deceived by their movement
throughout the lands."[86]

* * * * * * *

Among the realities of faith and facts of life is this: the
true adherents to the Straight Path of Allāh (*aṣ-ṣirāṭ al-mustaqeem*)
are a small minority, living as strangers in society. The reason
is none other than the deviation of most of mankind from that
Path and their excessive attachment to this world. The Qur'ān
describes the majority of the earth's population:

﴿وَلَٰكِنَّ أَكْثَرَ النَّاسِ لَايَعْلَمُونَ﴾

"But most of the people do not know."[87]

﴿بَلْ أَكْثَرُهُم لَايَعْقِلُونَ﴾

"No, but most of them do not use their minds."[88]

﴿أَكْثَرَ النَّاسِ لَايُؤْمِنُونَ﴾

"Most of the people do not believe."[89]

﴿إِن هُم إِلَّا كَالأَنْعَامِ بَل هُم أَضَلُّ﴾

"They are not except like sheep. No, but they
are even more astray."[90]

---

[86] *Sūrah Ghāfir*, 40:4. Activities not disciplined by fear of Allāh may
appear impressive but are, in fact, void of blessing in this life and the next.
[87] *Sūrah Yūsuf*, 12:21.
[88] *Sūrah al-'Ankabūt*, 29:63.
[89] *Sūrah Ghāfir*, 40:59.
[90] *Sūrah al-Furqān*, 25:44.

The degree of alienation varies from time to time, place to place, people to people – for Muslims are a minority among the inhabitants of this earth, and believers are a minority among Muslims. Those of knowledge are few among believers, and those defending the Prophet's *sunnah* are even fewer. In respect to this, the Messenger of Allāh (ﷺ) said, "Verily, my community among communities is like a white hair on a black bull."[91]

Although they may find comfort in solitude and suffer isolation in the company of those who seek only to socialize, these servants cannot neglect their duties because the Prophet (ﷺ) declared, "The believer who mixes with people and is patient in the face of their offense is preferable to the believer who does not mix with people and is not patient with their offense."[92] And Allāh reminds them:

﴿إِنَّمَا الْمُؤْمِنُونَ إِخْوَةٌ﴾

"The believers are but brothers."[93]

So how can one avoid his brother for whom he cares and shares responsibility?

Always aware of Allāh's presence, however, such souls seldom seek companionship elsewhere, knowing that He alone can comprehend their concerns, appreciate their efforts and relieve their sorrows. And knowing that whatever the people might think, Allāh enumerates and rewards that which is unnoticed – sincerity of intention, conscientiousness in deed, and pain born patiently in the heart. So these servants of Allāh are careful to avoid what is doubtful or might possibly lead to *ḥarām* (that which is unlawful) and are indifferent to that which is of no benefit in the Hereafter. They fear Allāh when dealing

---

[91] Al-Bukhārī.
[92] Aḥmad and at-Tirmidhī – *ṣaḥeeḥ*.
[93] ***Sūrah al-Ḥujurāt,*** 49:10.

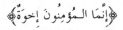

with others and even more so when dealing with the subtle affairs of their own hearts. They refuse to compromise *tawḥeed,* and seek opportunities for *jihād.* They cling to the *sunnah* when people have abandoned it and avoid innovation in religion while people find it good. They know the gravity of their sins and strive for forgiveness from their Lord. They are the ones whom the Prophet (ﷺ) praised when he said, "Certainly Islām began as [something] alien, and it will become alien once again as it began. So, blessed are the aliens."[94]

Yet, human souls were created as social beings with a natural enjoyment of companionship and feelings of loneliness during periods of isolation. Therefore, Allāh (*subḥānahu wa ta'ālā*) assures those who travel on His Path that, in spite of temporary alienation from contemporaries, they do belong to the best company of mankind – none other than the prophets, their supporters, the martyrs and the righteous.[95] Such is the reason for the supplication: "O Allāh, guide me among those You have guided."[96] Remembering one's companions removes sadness from the heart. Although they may be rare throughout the servant's lifetime, he can certainly look forward to a joyful reception in the Hereafter. Ibn al-Qayyim said, "Every time you feel the loneliness of isolation, remember your companions who have preceded you and be eager to join them; and do not be concerned with others, for they will not avail you at all before Allāh. And if they call out to you during your journey, do not turn to them, for whenever you respond to them, they will take you and set you in another direction." Some early scholars used to advise, "Keep fast to the path of truth, and do not succumb to loneliness because of the few who tread it; and beware of the path of falsehood, and do not be deceived by the

---

[94]Muslim and Aḥmad.
[95]See *Sūrah an-Nisā'*, 4:69.
[96]اللّٰهُمَّ اهدِنِي فِيمَن هَدَيتَ From *du'aa' ul-qunūt* taught by the Prophet (ﷺ). Related by an-Nasā'ī – *ḥasan.*

many headed on it to destruction." In the words of Allāh (*subḥānahu wa ta'ālā*):

﴿قُل لايَستَوِي الخَبِيثُ وَالطَّيِّبُ وَلَو أَعجَبَكَ كَثرَةُ الخَبِيثِ﴾

"Say, 'Not equal are evil and good, even if you are impressed by the abundance of evil.'" [97]

﴿وَإِن تُطِع أَكثَرَ مَن فِي الأَرضِ يُضِلُّوكَ عَن سَبِيلِ اللهِ إِن يَتَّبِعُونَ إِلاَّ الظَّنَّ وَإِن هُم إِلاَّ يَخرُصُونَ﴾

"And if you obey most of those on earth, they will lead you astray from the way of Allāh. They follow nothing but speculation, and they are not but those who falsify." [98]

In another sense, however, the believer shares the company of all those creations that worship and praise Allāh day and night throughout the universe, and thus, he is actually among the ranks of the majority of His creation.

﴿سَبَّحَ لِلَّهِ مَا فِي السَّمَاوَاتِ وَمَا فِي الأَرضِ﴾

"To Allāh gives praise that which is in the heavens and that which is on the earth." [99]

For in addition to that portion of *jinn* and mankind who worship Allāh, the animals and plants are worshipping and praising Him. All the angels filling the heavens worship Allāh. Seemingly inanimate bodies worship Allāh. All forms of energy and matter worship Allāh, submitting to the physical laws He has established for creation and praising Him in their own particular way.

---

[97] *Sūrah al-Mā'idah,* 5:100.
[98] *Sūrah al-An'ām,* 6:116.
[99] *Sūrahs* 59:1, 61:1, 62:1 and 64:1.

﴿وَإِن مِن شَيْءٍ إِلاَّ يُسَبِّحُ بِحَمْدِهِ وَلَـٰكِن لاتَفقَهُونَ تَسبِيحَهُم﴾

"And there is nothing that does not praise Him, but you do not understand their praise."[100]

Finally, and above all, Allāh Himself is with the righteous servant,[101] supporting his efforts and reassuring him.[102] So while Shayṭān will attempt to infect him with loneliness and despair, his plan is frustrated and defeated by the realization that the believer is in harmony with the entire universe in submission to the will of Allāh, whereas those who vainly try to oppose Him are but a small minority that will surely be overcome.

If the adherent to the Straight Path feels himself to be a stranger in this world, all men, in fact, are such. They were not created for this life but are merely travelers along the road to the final destination. So, whoever travels light, sending provisions on before him, will ease his burden and find his home in order upon arrival.

---

100 *Sūrah al-Isrā',* 17:44.

101 See *Sūrah an-Naḥl,* 16:128.

102 ﴿وَلا تَهِنُوا وَلاتَحزَنُوا وَأَنتُمُ الأَعلَونَ﴾ ***"Do not weaken or grieve while you are superior."*** (*Sūrah Āli 'Imrān,* 3:139)

﴿إِن تَكُونُوا تَألَمُونَ فَإِنَّهُم يَألَمُونَ كَمَا تَـألَمُونَ وَتَرجُـونَ مِـنَ اللهِ مَـا لايَرجُـونَ﴾ ***"If you are suffering, they [too] are suffering, but you expect from Allāh that which they do not expect."*** (*Sūrah an-Nisā',* 4:104)

SUPPLICATION

(AD-DU‘AA’)

SUPPLICATION (AD-DU'AA')

﴿أَمَّن يُجِيبُ الْمُضْطَرَّ إِذَا دَعَاهُ وَيَكْشِفُ السُّوءَ﴾

"Who is it that responds to the desperate one when he calls upon Him, and removes evil?" [103]

* * * * * * *

Supplication to Allāh is ordered by Him, and He promises response:

﴿ادعُونِي أَستَجِب لَكُم﴾

"Call upon Me; I will answer you." [104]

﴿وَإِذَا سَأَلَكَ عِبَادِي عَنِّي فَإِنِّي قَرِيبٌ أُجِيبُ دَعوَةَ الدَّاعِ إِذَا دَعَانِ﴾

"And if My servants ask you about Me – certainly I am near. I answer the prayer of the supplicant when he calls upon Me." [105]

Du'aa' is encouraged not only in formal prayer (*ṣalāh*) but at any other time one is inclined to it. It is an important form of worship and is evidence of one's belief in the power and ability of the Almighty. It is an open line of communication between the servant and his Lord; and by its constant practice, awareness of Him is sustained, and one joins the ranks of:

﴿وَالذَّاكِرِينَ اللهَ كَثِيرًا وَالذَّاكِرَاتِ﴾

"...the men and women who remember Allāh often." [106]

---

103 *Sūrah an-Naml,* 27:62.
104 *Sūrah Ghāfir,* 40:60.
105 *Sūrah al-Baqarah,* 2:186.
106 *Sūrah al-Aḥzāb,* 33:35.

The Messenger of Allāh (ﷺ) said, "Whoever would be pleased to have Allāh respond to him during hardship and disaster should make much *du'aa'* in times of ease."[107] He also said, "Supplication is [true] worship."[108]

How many servants miss out on great opportunities for benefit in this world and the next by their ignorance of this subject. Indeed, every tool, every treatment, every means to an end has a proper use. When used in the correct manner, the desired result will be obtained by Allāh's permission, but improper use will accordingly lead to failure. In following the example of the Prophet (ﷺ) and his instructions, we can make the best use of *du'aa'*.

Facing the *qiblah* when possible, raising the hands to the shoulder level, stretching them out when there is urgency, and beginning with praise of Allāh are all part of the *sunnah* of *du'aa'*. One should try to take advantage of the times and conditions when response is most likely.[109] Indeed, the best manner of making *du'aa'* is for the servant to concentrate with all of his heart, show humility to Allāh and pray in a lowered voice, as Allāh orders:

﴿ادْعُوا رَبَّكُمْ تَضَرُّعًا وَخُفْيَةً إِنَّهُ لَا يُحِبُّ الْمُعْتَدِينَ﴾

"Call upon your Lord in humility and fear, [for] He does not like aggressors."[110]

Aggression in *du'aa'* was explained by scholars as shouting or showing off one's skill in the use of words.[111]

---

[107] At-Tirmidhī – *ḥasan.*

[108] Aḥmad, Abū Dāwūd, at-Tirmidhī and others – *ṣaḥeeḥ.*

[109] These include the following: the month of Ramadhān, the day of 'Arafah, Fridays, the last portion of the night (especially the last hour before dawn), between the *ādhaan* and the *iqāmah,* during prostration in prayer, immediately after obligatory prayers, when the armies meet during *jihād,* and at any times of fear or sensitivity of the heart.

[110] *Sūrah al-A'rāf,* 7:55.

[111] Group supplication led by one person while others repeat after him →

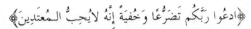

Upon hearing people raising their voices in *du'aa'*, the Messenger of Allāh (ﷺ) said, "O people, return to yourselves. You do not call upon someone who is deaf or absent but rather, One who is Hearing and Seeing. The One you call upon is nearer to one of you than the neck of the beast he rides."[112]

Be certain that Allāh responds willingly, and ask Him accordingly, as the Prophet (ﷺ) said, "Let not one of you say, 'O Allāh, forgive me, if You will' because there is no unwillingness."[113] Additionally, he instructed, "If you ask Allāh, ask Him being certain of response."[114] He also informed us that there are three supplications which are not refused: that of the parent (for his child), that of the traveler, and that of the oppressed (against his oppressor).[115] Another *ḥadīth* affirms that the *du'aa'* of a person for his brother Muslim who is absent from him is also answered.[116] The Messenger of Allāh (ﷺ) directed that when supplicating for another, one should begin with himself,[117] saying, for example, "O Allāh, guide me and guide him," or "O Allāh, forgive me and forgive him."

There are certain things to be avoided in relation to *du'aa'* as they prevent response from Allāh (*subḥānahu wa ta'ālā*). *Du'aa'* must not be made for anything sinful or for cutting off relations. The Prophet (ﷺ) said, "No Muslim prays to Allāh with a *du'aa'* free from sin and from that which cuts ties between relatives without Allāh giving him one of three things:

---

is an innovation and was not practiced by the Prophet (ﷺ) or his companions. Individual *du'aa'* is preferable, or one may join the *du'aa'* of another by saying "*āmeen*" at the end.

112 Al-Bukhārī and Muslim.

113 Al-Bukhārī and Abū Dāwūd.

114 Aḥmad, Muslim and al-Bukhārī.

115 Abū Dāwūd and at-Tirmidhī – *ḥasan.*

116 Muslim.

117 At-Tirmidhī – *ṣaḥeeḥ.*

the answer to his prayer during his lifetime, the accumulation of its reward for him until the next life, or the prevention of some evil from striking him which is equal to it [i.e., his effort in *du'aa'*]."[118] Allāh (*subḥānahu wa ta'ālā*) is well aware of which one of the three responses is most beneficial to the servant. One should not demand an immediate response, as he who says, "I prayed but was not answered" and then gives up.[119] The Prophet (ﷺ) also forbade making *du'aa'* against oneself, one's family, property or servants.[120] Moreover, the supplicant must not be a consumer of *ḥarām* (that which is unlawful). The Messenger of Allāh (ﷺ) mentioned a man on a long journey – all dirty and dusty – raising his hands to Heaven, saying, "O Lord, O Lord" while his food was from *ḥarām*, his clothing from *ḥarām* and his having been sustained by *ḥarām*. He (ﷺ) concluded, "How then could he have been answered?"[121]

A consideration of *du'aa'* inevitably leads to the question of fate (*al-qadr*) and the relationship between the two. Among the best discussions of this subject is one presented by Imām Ibn al-Qayyim in *Al-Jawāb ul-Kāfi*.

Ibn Qayyim al-Jawziyyah was asked, "What do the scholars say about a man who has been tried with affliction – knowing that if it continues it will ruin him in this life and in the next – and has tried everything in his ability to get rid of it, but it only increases in severity? What is the method of warding it off? May Allāh have mercy upon him who helps an afflicted one; and Allāh is in assistance of the servant as long as the servant is in assistance of his brother..."

The *shaykh* answered:[122] *Al-ḥamdu-lillāh.* It has been confirmed in *Ṣaḥeeḥ al-Bukhārī* that the Prophet (ﷺ) said,

---

118 Aḥmad – *ḥasan.*

119 Al-Bukhārī, Muslim, at-Tirmidhī and Abū Dāwūd.

120 Muslim.

121 Muslim and al-Bukhārī.

122 What remains of this chapter is a summary of Ibn al-Qayyim's words.

"Allāh has sent down no disease for which He has not sent down a cure." And it is documented in *Ṣaḥeeḥ Muslim* that the Prophet (ﷺ) said, "For every disease there is a medicine; and when the medicine contacts the disease, it cures with the permission of Allāh." This includes the diseases of the heart and soul, as well as the body, and their treatments. The Prophet (ﷺ) considered ignorance a disease and consulting the learned as its treatment. Allāh (*subḥānahu wa ta'ālā*) informs us that the Qur'ān is a cure:

﴿قُلْ هُوَ لِلَّذِينَ آمَنُوا هُدًى وَشِفَاءٌ﴾

> ***"Say, 'It is, for those who have believed, a guidance and cure.'"*** [123]

﴿وَنُنَزِّلُ مِنَ الْقُرْآنِ مَا هُوَ شِفَاءٌ وَرَحْمَةٌ لِلْمُؤْمِنِينَ﴾

> ***"And We reveal of the Qur'ān that which is a cure and a mercy for the believers."*** [124]

In fact, the Qur'ān is a cure for hearts from the diseases of ignorance and doubt.

And such also is *du'aa'*, for it is one of the most powerful causes of warding off anything disliked or of obtaining that which is desired. It is possible, however, that the desired effect might not follow, due either to a weakness in the *du'aa'* itself – such as one not liked by Allāh because it contains aggression – or to half-heartedness in the supplicant. The failure could be due as well to a factor which prevents response such as the supplicant's consumption of *ḥarām* or the control of his heart by earthly lusts or distractions.

Indeed, *du'aa'* is one of the most beneficial medicines. It is the enemy of disaster – defending against it and fighting it, preventing its descent and pushing it back, and weakening it if

---

[123] *Sūrah Fuṣṣilat*, 41:44.
[124] *Sūrah al-Isrā'*, 17:82.

it should descend. It is the weapon of the believer.

When *du'aa'* meets disaster, there are three possibilities:

1. The *du'aa'* is stronger than the disaster and thus drives it away.
2. The *du'aa'* is weaker than the disaster, so the disaster overcomes and the servant is struck (although it may be lessened in degree by even a weak *du'aa'*).
3. The *du'aa'* and the disaster oppose each other, and each one prevents the other from victory. The Prophet (ﷺ) said, "Nothing repels fate except *du'aa'*."[125] And among the best of treatments is persistence in *du'aa'*. The Prophet (ﷺ) said, "Do not weaken in *du'aa'*, for no one will be destroyed as long as he is making *du'aa'*."[126]

Among the weaknesses which prevent the effect of *du'aa'* is haste or impatience. According to the Prophet (ﷺ), "Any one of you will be answered as long as he is not hasty, saying, 'I made *du'aa'*, but it was not answered.'"[127] When the Prophet (ﷺ) said, "The servant continues to be answered as long as he does not ask for something sinful or for that which cuts ties between relatives, and as long as he is not impatient," he was asked, "O Messenger of Allāh, what is impatience?" He replied, "Impatience is when one says, 'I prayed and prayed, but I do not see that I am being answered,' and so becoming tired, abandons *du'aa'*."[128] So the servant should not give up *du'aa'* prematurely, thinking the answer to be slow in coming; for then he becomes like one who plants a seed or a twig and begins to care for it and water it, but when he finds it to be slow in growing, leaves it and neglects it.

---

125 At-Tirmidhī and al-Ḥākim – *ḥasan.*
126 Al-Ḥākim, who graded it *ṣaḥeeḥ.*
127 Al-Bukhārī.
128 Muslim.

Therefore, if *du'aa'* is combined with presence of heart and complete concentration on what is desired, and it corresponds with one of the times when response is expected, and it is accompanied by fear of Allāh, humbleness and humility to Him, in earnest and in gentleness, and then the supplicant faces the *qiblah,* and is in a state of purity (*ṭahārah*), and then raises his hands to Allāh, beginning with praise of Him and blessings upon the Prophet (ﷺ), and asks forgiveness and repents, then supplicates, begging Allāh and persisting in his request in fear and hope, using the best names of Allāh and words recited by the Prophet – all this after having offered some charity (*ṣadaqah*) – such a *du'aa'* could hardly be refused at all; and this is the kind most pleasing to Allāh (*subḥānahu wa ta'ālā*).

Often it becomes known that people have used a certain *du'aa'* and were answered. But it must also be realized that accompanying that *du'aa'* was urgent need and sincere turning to Allāh. Or perhaps there was some good that one had done previously, or the *du'aa'* was made at one of the hours of response, or there was some other reason for which it was answered. Therefore, one might think that the secret was in the wording of the *du'aa'* and subsequently use it without the other factors being present. Such is the case in which a man uses a good medicine at the proper time and in the proper way and thus benefits from it. Others might think that simply using that medicine is sufficient to cure under any circumstance, but they are mistaken. Similarly, if a supplication happens to be near a grave, an ignorant person might assume that the secret is in the grave, unaware that it is actually in the supplicant's urgency and sincerity when turning to Allāh. But when *du'aa'* is made in a mosque (*masjid*), it is better and more pleasing to Allāh.

Prayer is like a sword; and the effectiveness of a sword is in its use by the swordsman. So, when the sword is perfect, without fault, when the swordsman's arm is strong and skillful, and when no preventing factor is present, then the enemy is defeated. But if one of these three conditions is weak, then the effect is weakened accordingly. Thus if one's *du'aa'* is not a proper one or one's heart is not combined with his tongue therein or a prohibiting factor (such as disobedience) is present, then the effect will not be obtained.

There is a well-known argument that states: "If the effect of *du'aa'* has been decreed, then it must happen whether the servant asks for it or not; and if it was not decreed, then it will not happen in any case." A certain group, believing this opinion to be correct, stopped making *du'aa'*, saying that there is no use in it; but they, in their excessive ignorance and deviation, contradict themselves. For if this school of thought was to be followed, it would necessitate the annulment of all causes. Thus, if relief from hunger and thirst was decreed for one, it would happen whether or not he ate or drank; and if a child was decreed for one, there would be no need for him to approach his wife; and so on. Would any sane person say such a thing? Even dumb animals instinctively apply themselves to the causes of their life and subsistence, so they are certainly smarter than those who make such unsubstantiated assertions.

Some, pretending intellect, have said, "Keeping busy with *du'aa'* is a form of worship rewarded by Allāh, but it has nothing to do with what is gained." So, to such people, the worldly result is the same whether one prays for something or remains silent. And others even more "intellectual" have said, "*Du'aa'* is not a cause but simply a sign that the servant's request is being granted." This is like saying that a black cloud is a sign of rain but not a cause of rain – the two only being present simultaneously!

The truth is actually in a third explanation – whatever is decreed is decreed by reason of causes. Nothing is decreed without a cause, and *du'aa'* is among the principal causes. So, whenever a servant applies the cause, then that which is decreed happens; and whenever he does not apply the cause, then it does not happen. Just as relief from hunger and thirst is decreed by reason of eating and drinking, and the birth of a child by reason of marital relations, and the growth of plants by sowing seeds, and the death of an animal by slaughter, and the entrance into Paradise by deeds, and into Hellfire by deeds... This is the true answer.

Du'aa' [combined with other efforts] is among the strongest of causes, and nothing is more beneficial or more far-reaching in obtaining the need. Just as the Prophet's companions (may Allāh be pleased with them) were the most knowledgeable of the community in respect to the religion, so were they more steadfast than others in applying this cause with its conditions and proper manners. 'Umar bin al-Khaṭṭāb used it against his enemies, and he was the greatest of soldiers. He used to tell his companions, "You will not be helped by [great] numbers, but you will be helped from Heaven."

We have been led by the mind and the instinct and then by history to recognize that righteousness is among the greatest causes for obtaining good upon this earth, and its opposite is among the greatest causes for obtaining evil. Allāh (*subḥānahu wa ta'ālā*) has made the reward or punishment of the Hereafter depend upon deeds which are conditions, the effect depending upon the cause. In over 1,000 places throughout the Qur'ān an event or result is tied to its cause in descriptions of both this life and the next.

Anyone who understands this fact will benefit greatly. He will not sit passively waiting for fate to overtake him. One with understanding will answer fate with fate and will oppose fate with fate. For indeed, hunger is fate and thirst is fate and cold is fate and fear is fate; yet all creatures exert themselves to change that fate. And that is what Allāh has willed.

In order for one to take full advantage of this knowledge, two things are necessary:

1. The servant must learn the causes of good and evil, developing such an understanding from all that he observes around him, from what he has experienced,

from what others have experienced, and from what he has heard about other peoples, both ancient and modern. For this purpose, nothing is better than the study of the Qur'ān and *ḥadīth,* since they picture good and evil and their causes to the reader almost as though he were an eyewitness. Then a look into history will provide the details within the general outlines given by Allāh and His Messenger (ﷺ).

2. The servant must beware of himself being a preventing factor, blocking the desired result. Knowing that disobedience and ignorance are definite causes of harm to him in this life and the next, he should seek to remedy this in himself, not only to escape penalty in the Hereafter but also to obtain the maximum result when he turns to Allāh in *du'aa'* throughout his life on earth.

DEATH

(AL-MAWT)

DEATH (AL-MAWT)

﴿كُلُّ نَفسٍ ذَائِقَةُ المَوتِ﴾

"Every soul will taste death."[129]

* * * * * * *

Almost everyday we see or hear of a death, often that of someone we know; yet how often do we consider our own time and what will follow? While a funeral procession passes before us, we admit that, true, death has come to others; but we are still here and feel that we will continue to be for a long time. Once when a funeral procession passed near the Prophet (ﷺ), he remarked, "Relieved or relieved of him." Some inquired, "What is the meaning of 'relieved' and 'relieved of him'?" He answered, "The believing servant is relieved of the fatigue and afflictions of this world, [entering] into the mercy of Allāh; and people, countries, plants and animals are relieved of the transgressing servant."[130]

Consider a person who expects to travel and how he thinks of nothing but his journey – what to take along and how best to prepare himself. The believer prepares in the same way for his final and most important journey. This temporary station (i.e., life) in which he waits is not his primary concern. ‘Abdullāh bin ‘Umar reported that once the Messenger of Allāh (ﷺ) took hold of his shoulders and said, "Be in this world as a stranger or a traveler."[131] The One who has given life will surely take it back at the time determined by Him. There is no destination but the return to Allāh, and there is no hope but in the acceptance of Allāh. It is death which exposes the truth about this life – everything material will be left behind. For

---

[129] *Sūrahs* 3:185, 21:35 and 29:57.
[130] Al-Bukhārī and Muslim.
[131] Al-Bukhārī.

those who love the comforts of worldly life, it is good to remember the harshness and solitude of the grave and that one will be removed irrevocably from all that to which he had been so closely attached. The Prophet (ﷺ) advised, "Remember often the destroyer of pleasures – death."[132]

Death is an awesome reality facing every living being. It is, in itself, a severe trial. Even Prophet Muḥammad (ﷺ), the most beloved of Allāh's creatures, was not spared its agony. For the believer, affliction at death (as at any time) is a means of expiating sins or gaining a higher position in Paradise. Those attending a dying person should make every effort to have him remember Allāh and give him hope and reassurance, not allowing him to submit to Shayṭān out of pain or fear. The Prophet (ﷺ) said, "Help your dying ones to say, 'لا إله إلا الله' ('Lā ilāha ill-Allāh.')."[133] And he also reported, "When death draws near to the believer, he receives glad tidings of Allāh's pleasure with him and His generosity, so nothing is more loved by him than what is before him. As for the companion of the Fire, whose deeds were sealed with evil, he is given the news of it [i.e., Hellfire] during this terror [of death]."[134]

In the Qur'ān, Allāh (subḥānahu wa ta'ālā) gives a clear description of what happens at that time:

$$﴿وَلَوْ تَرَىٰ إِذْ يَتَوَفَّى الَّذِينَ كَفَرُوا الْمَلَائِكَةُ يَضْرِبُونَ وُجُوهَهُمْ وَأَدْبَارَهُمْ وَذُوقُوا عَذَابَ الْحَرِيقِ ذَٰلِكَ بِمَا قَدَّمَتْ أَيْدِيكُمْ وَأَنَّ اللَّهَ لَيْسَ بِظَلَّامٍ لِلْعَبِيدِ﴾$$

"If [only] you could see when the angels take the souls of those who disbelieved, striking

---

132At-Tirmidhī, an-Nasā'ī and Ibn Mājah – *ṣaḥeeḥ*.

133Muslim, Abū Dāwūd and at-Tirmidhī. Scholars have added that this should be a gentle encouragement without insistence if it is feared that the person might become upset. It could be said by someone else within hearing distance to serve as an indirect reminder to the dying.

134Al-Bukhārī.

their faces and backs and [saying], 'Taste the punishment of the Fire.' That is for what your hands have put forth [of evil deeds]; and never is Allāh unjust to His servants." [135]

﴿إِنَّ الَّذِينَ قَالُوا رَبُّنَا اللهُ ثُمَّ اسْتَقَامُوا تَتَنَزَّلُ عَلَيْهِمُ الْمَلَائِكَةُ أَلَّا تَخَافُوا وَلَا تَحْزَنُوا وَأَبْشِرُوا بِالْجَنَّةِ الَّتِي كُنتُمْ تُوعَدُونَ﴾

"Those who have said, 'Our Lord is Allāh' and then have become upright – the angels will descend upon them, [saying], 'Do not fear nor be sad, but receive good news of the Paradise which you were promised.'" [136]

Death is an awakening after a dream – lucidity after confusion. It is a second birth into a greater life. If the life of this world was created for work and trial, then the life of the next world was created for judgement and lasting compensation.

At death the soul leaves the body. All things are now absolutely clear to that soul – the realities concerning all of which one was unaware during his lifetime or chose to ignore.[137] The Messenger of Allāh (ﷺ) reported, "When one of you dies, he is shown his place [in the Hereafter] morning and evening. If he is from the people of Heaven, then among the people of Heaven. And if he is from the people of Hell, then among the people of Hell. And it will be said to him, 'This is your place until Allāh resurrects you on the Day of Judgement.'"[138] Thus each soul remains until the Day of Judgement (according to its preview of the Hereafter), feeling sadness and regret or happiness and reassurance.

---

[135] *Sūrah al-Anfāl,* 8:50-51.
[136] *Sūrah Fuṣṣilat,* 41:30.
[137] See *Sūrah Qāf,* 50:20.
[138] Al-Bukhārī and Muslim.

"The grave is the first station among the stations of the Hereafter."[139] In a long and detailed *ḥadīth* the Prophet (ﷺ) described how two angels come to the believer in beautiful form, taking his sweet-smelling soul gently up to the seventh heaven where Allāh registers him and the angels question him about his Lord, his religion and his prophet. After he has answered correctly, "My Lord is Allāh; my religion is Islām; and my prophet is Muḥammad (ﷺ)," his soul is returned to its body in the grave, which is expanded for him for as far as he can see. Then his good deeds come to keep him company in the form of a beautiful man telling him to look forward to all that will please him. As for the disbeliever, two angels come to him in ugly form, tearing his foul-smelling soul violently from its body; and when they ascend to the lowest of the heavens, the door does not open, and Allāh registers him in the book of Hell. His soul is then thrown back to its body in the grave, and the angels come to question him about his Lord, his religion and his prophet. But he can only answer, "Uh... uh... I don't know." (And in another narration: "I only said as the people said.") So the door of Hell is opened before him, and his grave contracts, compressing him until his ribs are crushed against each other. Then his bad deeds come to him in the form of a disgusting man telling him to look forward to all that he despises – humiliation and eternal punishment – and he is struck a blow which causes his scream to be heard by everything except men and *jinn.*[140] The Prophet (ﷺ) advised us to seek from Allāh protection from the punishment of the grave and the punishment of the Fire.[141]

All this, and the Day of Judgement has not yet arrived! In truth, one's reward or punishment begins from the instant of death, when he leaves the familiar confines of time and space.

---

[139] At-Tirmidhī – *ḥasan.*

[140] Aḥmad – *ṣaḥeeḥ.*

[141] Al-Bukhārī and Muslim.

﴿إِنَّهُمْ يَرَوْنَهُ بَعِيدًا وَنَرَاهُ قَرِيبًا﴾

"Certainly, they see it as distant, but We see it as near."[142]

The reality of death is that it is simply a stage in man's development, as birth was – a transition from one world to another. Knowledge of this fact given to the Muslim is another example of Allāh's endless mercy upon him, for with this knowledge he can prepare himself for success.

The Qur'ān is explicit in its statement that no one but Allāh knows when the appointed Hour will be:

﴿قُلْ إِنَّمَا عِلْمُهَا عِندَ رَبِّي لاَ يُجَلِّيهَا لِوَقْتِهَا إِلاَّ هُوَ﴾

"Say, 'Its knowledge is only with my Lord. No one can expose its time except Him.'"[143]

Certain signs or warnings have been mentioned in both the Qur'ān and the prophetic statements – events that will take place before that Last Hour; but these signs are for the living to observe. The souls of the dead are no longer subject to time as we know it. The Prophet (ﷺ) once said, "The Hour will not come until 'Allāh, Allāh' is no longer uttered upon the earth," (i.e., when Allāh [*subḥānahu wa ta'ālā*] has been completely forgotten by the earth's inhabitants.)[144]

Just as the death of every individual is the first stage in his new life, the death of the universe and its recreation in a different form signals the beginning of the true existence promised by Allāh:[145]

---

[142] *Sūrah al-Ma'ārij,* 70:6-7.

[143] *Sūrah al-A'rāf,* 7:187.

[144] Muslim. At that point there will no longer be any reason for continuation of the present creation. It must make way for the new order.

[145] ﴿وَإِنَّ الدَّارَ الآخِرَةَ لَهِيَ الحَيَوَانُ لَوْ كَانُوا يَعْلَمُونَ﴾ ***"But truly the home of the Hereafter is the actual life, if only they knew."*** (*Sūrah al-'Ankabūt,* 29:64)

﴿كَمَا بَدَأْنَا أَوَّلَ خَلْقٍ نُعِيدُهُ وَعْدًا عَلَيْنَا إِنَّا كُنَّا فَاعِلِينَ﴾

"As We began the first creation, We will repeat it. [That is] a promise binding upon Us. Certainly will We carry it out." [146]

﴿يَوْمَ تُبَدَّلُ الأَرْضُ غَيْرَ الأَرْضِ وَالسَّمَاوَاتُ﴾

"On a Day when the earth will be replaced by another earth, and the heavens [as well]..." [147]

When the appointed Hour has arrived, the whole universe will undergo such drastic changes as no man can imagine. In early Makkan *sūrahs,* Allāh (*subḥānahu wa ta'ālā*) gives terrifying descriptions of some of these events in order to awaken man and shake him into the realization that Allāh (*subḥānahu wa ta'ālā*) will manifest His absolute power and control that Day over all things, that He will restore life to the dead, and that all beings will be then totally helpless and answerable to Him...

﴿إِذَا السَّمَاءُ انفَطَرَتْ وَإِذَا الكَوَاكِبُ انتَثَرَتْ وَإِذَا البِحَارُ فُجِّرَتْ
وَإِذَا القُبُورُ بُعْثِرَتْ عَلِمَتْ نَفْسٌ مَا قَدَّمَتْ وَأَخَّرَتْ﴾

"When the sky is shattered and when the planets are scattered and when the seas are exploded and when the graves are exposed, then will a soul know what it has put forth and kept back." [148]

The Hour will be heralded by a trumpet blast which will strike everyone in the heavens and upon the earth dead from terror, except whom Allāh wills. Then upon the second blast,

---

146 *Sūrah al-Anbiyā',* 21:104.
147 *Sūrah Ibrāheem,* 14:48.
148 *Sūrah al-Infiṭār,* 82:1-5.

life will be restored to all of the dead.[149] Each will feel as one who has slept but a short while, having been awakened when the soul returned to the body.

﴿وَيَومَ تَقُومُ السَّاعَةُ يُقسِمُ المُجرِمُونَ مَا لَبِثُوا غَيرَ سَاعَةٍ﴾

"And the day the Hour is established, the criminals will swear that they had remained but an hour."[150]

Thus will every soul be returned to life in the same psychological condition it was at the time of death – in belief or denial, in good or evil. In support of this statement are the Prophet's words: "Every servant will be brought back to life in accordance with the state in which he died."[151]

The second creation of man will occur in a way similar to the growth of plants upon the earth. Allāh (*subḥānahu wa ta'ālā*) points to this fact in the Qur'ān.[152] In authentic *ḥadīths* the Prophet (ﷺ) explained, "...then water will descend from the heavens, and they [i.e., people] will grow as vegetation grows. There is no part of man which will not have decayed except for one bone, which is the base of the tail,[153] from which creation will be developed on the Day of Judgement."[154] And he (ﷺ) said, "Every part of a son of Ādam is consumed by the earth except for the base of the tail. He was created from it, and he will be reassembled from it."[155]

All creatures will then be gathered together for the Judgement – men, *jinn,* even animals – each one alone, stripped of friends and family ties.

149See *Sūrah az-Zumar,* 39:68.
150*Sūrah ar-Rūm,* 30:55.
151Muslim.
152See *sūrahs* 30:19, 43:11 and 50:9-11.
153 *'Ajbudh-dhanab,* described as being like a grain or a mustard seed.
154Al-Bukhārī and Muslim.
155Muslim.

﴾فَلَا أَنسَابَ بَيْنَهُمْ يَوْمَئِذٍ﴿

"And no relationship will there be for them on that Day." [156]

The following information about the Gathering comes from *Saheeh Muslim*: People will be gathered on a land that is white, untrodden, pure and unowned by anyone. They will be gathered as they were at birth – barefoot, naked and uncircumcised – but they will be too preoccupied to notice each other. This Day every person will be concerned only with the judgement that awaits him, no longer thinking of those he loved in his earthly life – even being willing to sacrifice them to save himself, if only that was possible. [157] On that Day Allah (*subhānahu wa ta'ālā*) will fold up the heavens, taking them in His right hand; and He will fold up the earth, taking it in His left hand, saying, "I am the Sovereign. Where are the tyrants? Where are the arrogant?"

Then there will be the taking of account and the judgement. The justice that man instinctively longs for but never realizes in this earthly life will be established. And the justice of Allāh is complete, taking into account all deeds, intentions and conditions. Not one particle of good or evil will be ignored in His register.

﴾لَا يُغَادِرُ صَغِيرَةً وَلَا كَبِيرَةً إِلَّا أَحْصَاهَا﴿

"It leaves nothing small or great but that it was counted." [158]

﴾فَمَن يَعْمَلْ مِثْقَالَ ذَرَّةٍ خَيْرًا يَرَهُ وَمَن يَعْمَلْ مِثْقَالَ ذَرَّةٍ شَرًّا يَرَهُ﴿

---

[156] *Sūrah al-Mu'minūn*, 23:101.
[157] See *Sūrah al-Ma'ārij*, 70:11-14.
[158] *Sūrah al-Kahf*, 18:49.

*"Whoever does an atom's weight of good will
see it, and whoever does an atom's weight of
evil will see it."* [159]

Everyone will be perfectly convinced of the justice of his
judgement, and the balance will prove to him without a doubt
what he deserves. Indeed, nothing will benefit him this Day
except the good which he had put forth in his former life and
the mercy and forgiveness of Allāh, which he hopes for now.
For even the intercession of the Prophet will be only by Allāh's
permission.

Every servant will be given his record, published openly
before all creation, and he will be told:

﴿اقْرَأْ كِتَابَكَ كَفَى بِنَفْسِكَ الْيَوْمَ عَلَيْكَ حَسِيبًا﴾

*"Read your record. Sufficient as an accountant
against you today is yourself."* [160]

The successful person on that Day will feel proud and
happy before his Lord and before all of creation, but the one
who is exposed and scandalized will have no escape from
humiliation. He will try to defend himself through lying as he
did in his earthly life.

﴿فَيَحْلِفُونَ لَهُ كَمَا يَحْلِفُونَ لَكُمْ﴾

"And they will swear to Him as they swear to you." [161]

And they will say:

﴿وَاللهِ رَبِّنَا مَا كُنَّا مُشْرِكِينَ﴾

*"By Allāh, our Lord, we were not mushrikeen
[those who associate others with Allāh]."* [162]

---

[159] *Sūrah az-Zalzalah*, 99:7-8.
[160] *Sūrah al-Isrā'*, 17:14.
[161] *Sūrah al-Mujādilah*, 58:18.
[162] *Sūrah al-An'ām*, 6:23.

But Allāh will silence their tongues, and as it is reported in the Qur'ān, their hands and feet – even their skins – will testify to the truth, leaving them with no further argument. Left with only sorrow, regret and self-hatred, they will be addressed:

$$﴿لَمَقْتُ ا للهِ أَكْبَرُ مِن مَّقْتِكُم أَنفُسَكُمْ﴾$$

"Allāh's hatred of you is even greater than your hatred of yourselves." [163]

Certainly has He prepared for them a just and fitting punishment for their crimes.

Concerning the believer who had sinned at times, the Messenger of Allāh (ﷺ) related that he will be confronted privately by his Lord, who will say, "Do you know that you have committed such and such a sin," mentioning each sin one by one until the servant has admitted all of them and sees that he can only be doomed to destruction. Then Allāh will say, "I had concealed it for you in the world, and I forgive you for it today." Then he will be given his record containing only the good that he did. As for the disbelievers and the hypocrites, the witnesses will say:

$$﴿هَٰؤُلَاءِ الَّذِينَ كَذَبُوا عَلَى رَبِّهِم أَلَا لَعْنَةُ ا للهِ عَلَى الظَّالِمِينَ﴾$$

"Those are the ones who lied against their Lord. May the curse of Allāh be upon the unjust." [164]

Such will be their reckoning. Everyone, believers and non-believers alike, will be exposed to Hell, approaching it and observing it at close range.

$$﴿وَإِن مِّنكُم إِلَّا وَارِدُهَا﴾$$

"And there is none of you except he will come before it." [165]

---

[163] *Sūrah Ghāfir,* 40:10.
[164] Al-Bukhārī and Muslim. The Qur'ānic reference is *Sūrah Hūd,* 11:18.
[165] *Sūrah Maryam,* 19:71.

Ḥadīths from *Ṣaḥeeḥ Muslim* and *Ṣaḥeeḥ al-Bukhārī* explain that a narrow bridge will be erected over Hell, and everyone will be made to pass over it. The best of the people will cross it at the speed of lightening, others at the speed of the wind, others at the speed of horses, and others will cross it more slowly, some crawling on their hands and knees. The wrongdoers and the unjust will not succeed in crossing it but will be seized by claws like giant thorns along the path, pulling them off of it into the Fire. Some of the believers will escape untouched, others narrowly escaping after having been scratched. Then those successful in crossing will proceed on to Paradise.

﴿يَوْمَ نَقُولُ لِجَهَنَّمَ هَلِ امْتَلَأْتِ وَتَقُولُ هَلْ مِن مَّزِيدٍ وَأُزْلِفَتِ
الْجَنَّةُ لِلْمُتَّقِينَ غَيْرَ بَعِيدٍ هَٰذَا مَا تُوعَدُونَ لِكُلِّ أَوَّابٍ حَفِيظٍ مَّنْ
خَشِيَ الرَّحْمَٰنَ بِالْغَيْبِ وَجَاءَ بِقَلْبٍ مُّنِيبٍ﴾

"...on the Day We will say to Hellfire, 'Have you been filled?' and it will say, 'Are there some more?' And Paradise will be brought near to the righteous, not far. 'This is what you were promised,' [will be said] to everyone who turns back [in repentance to Allāh] and keeps to His ordinance – those who feared Allāh when unseen and came with a repentant heart." [166]

There are detailed accounts of Hellfire and of Paradise in both the Qur'ān and the *sunnah,* informing us that the consequences of our actions and intentions will be both physical and emotional. These descriptions serve to bring the concept closer to man's understanding, yet it is perceived that the realities of the next life are greater than the human mind

---

[166] ***Sūrah Qāf,*** 50:30-33.

can comprehend. The eternal yet unbearable tortures of the Hellfire await those who have denied their Lord. Their efforts to escape will be futile, and their pleas for relief will be ignored. The punishment they will have earned for themselves by their rebellion and tyranny upon the earth will be the ultimate justice. The righteous believers who have worked hard, seeking the acceptance of Allāh, will be rewarded accordingly by forgiveness for their minor sins and entrance into Paradise, where they will have all that their souls desire, and more – the presence of the Lord Himself, who will be eternally pleased with them.

The Messenger of Allāh (ﷺ) once recited from the Qur'ān: *"For those who do good is good, and extra..."*[167] and then said, "When the people of Paradise have entered Paradise and the people of Hell have entered Hell, a crier will call out, 'O people of Paradise, you have a promise from Allāh, and He wishes to fulfill it for you.' So they will say, 'What could it be? Has He not made our scales heavy [with good deeds], whitened our faces [i.e., shown us in the best light], and caused us to enter Paradise and avoid Hellfire?' Then the screen will be removed, and they will look at Allāh. He will not have given them anything that they love more than looking at Him, and that is the 'extra.'"[168] Allāh Himself confirms:

﴿وُجُوهٌ يَوْمَئِذٍ نَاضِرَةٌ إِلَى رَبِّهَا نَاظِرَةٌ﴾

"Some faces on that Day will be bright, looking at their Lord."[169]

It is mentioned in the prophetic traditions that there are those among the believers who will enter the Fire for a time due to the gravity of their sins. It is possible that one might not be forgiven if he did not repent before his death. It is true, as

---

167 ***Sūrah Yūnus,*** 10:26. ﴿لِلَّذِينَ أَحْسَنُوا الْحُسْنَى وَزِيَادَةٌ﴾

168 Muslim.

169 ***Sūrah al-Qiyāmah,*** 75:22-23.

well, that every soul will be compensated in full at the time of judgement, and that even animals will obtain their rights. So if one has been unjust to others, then he has, in reality, been unjust to himself since he will have to pay the price. The Prophet (ﷺ) referred to such a person as "bankrupt" because he will come forward on the Day of Judgement with some good deeds, such as prayer, fasting and *zākah,* but if he had wronged others during his lifetime, those people will all take their compensation from his good deeds until, when there are no good deeds left, they will unload their bad deeds upon him, one by one, until justice is restored. Thus he will be thrown into the Fire.[170] The Prophet (ﷺ) added, "As for the true people of the Fire, they will not die therein nor will they live. But others of you afflicted by the Fire by reason of sins will be caused by Allāh to die therein a death[171] until, after their having become charcoal, permission will be given for intercession. They will then be gathered, brought forth and scattered in the rivers of Paradise. Then it will be said, 'O people of Paradise, pour upon them,' and they will grow like seeds that have been carried by a flood."[172]

Those who have loved the Messenger of Allāh, following his teachings and obeying him, can hope for his intercession in the life to come, for he said, "For every prophet there is a supplication which is answered. Every other prophet asked for

---

[170]Muslim.

[171]The word "*imātah*" (death) is used here in the sense of a temporary death or a sleep. It has been related in *Ṣaḥeeḥ al-Bukhārī* and *Ṣaḥeeḥ Muslim* that on the Day of Judgement a plump ram will be brought forth, which will be recognized as death by the inhabitants of Paradise and the Hellfire alike. The ram will be slaughtered before them, and they will be told, "O people of Paradise, [there is now] eternity and no death. O people of Hell, [there is now] eternity and no death." Thus their respective conditions of bliss or misery will be rendered complete.

[172]Muslim.

something immediate, but I have saved this prayer for my community until the Day of Judgement. And it will be obtained, Allāh willing, by whoever dies from my community not associating anything with Allāh."[173]

But lest a servant fall into false security, it must be emphasized that no one enters Paradise sooner or later without true belief and the proof of that belief, which is obedience to Allāh and His Prophet (ﷺ).[174] For it is stated in authentic *ḥadīths* that some Muslims will seek to join the Prophet at his pool but will be prevented, and Allāh will tell him (ﷺ), "Verily, you do not know what they did after you."[175] Indeed, Allāh (*subḥānahu wa ta'ālā*) warns about complacency in religion like that of the Jews and Christians, who claim that He has favored them over others. Concerning entry into Paradise, the Qur'ān states:

﴿لَيسَ بِأَمَانِيِّكُم وَلا أَمَانِيِّ أَهلِ الكِتَابِ مَن يَعمَل سُوءًا يُجزَ بِهِ
وَلَا يَجِدْ لَهُ مِن دُونِ اللهِ وَلِيًّا وَلَا نَصِيرًا﴾

> ***"It is not by your wishful thinking nor by the wishful thinking of the People of the Scriptures. Whoever does a wrong will be penalized for it, and he will not find for himself other than Allāh as protector or helper."*** [176]

In the Qur'ān, Allāh gives a picture of both sides of the Hereafter in order that the believer may attain a healthy balance between fear and hope; for certainly, an excess of either, in the form of despair or excessive optimism, is a deterrent to effort. Every Muslim must be aware that his fate is in his own hands

---

[173] Muslim. The Prophet (ﷺ) emphasized here that *tawḥeed* is a condition for his intercession.

[174] See *Sūrah Āli 'Imrān,* 3:31-32.

[175] Muslim.

[176] *Sūrah an-Nisā',* 4:123.

by the will of Allāh and that what awaits him in the life to come depends completely upon himself in this time of examination.

﴿كُلُّ نَفْسٍ ذَائِقَةُ الْـمَوْتِ وَإِنَّمَا تُوَفَّوْنَ أُجُورَكُم يَوْمَ الْقِيَامَةِ فَمَن زُحْزِحَ عَنِ النَّارِ وَأُدْخِلَ الْجَنَّةَ فَقَد فَازَ وَمَا الْحَيَاةُ الدُّنْيَا إلا مَتَاعُ الْغُرُورِ﴾

"Every soul will taste death, and only on the Day of Judgement will you be given what you earned. So, he who is prevented from the Fire and admitted to Paradise has attained his desire. And what is the life of this world except the enjoyment of deception..." [177]

---

[177] *Sūrah Āli 'Imrān*, 3:185.

AFTERWORD: A RETURN TO TAWḤEED

The *kalimah* (word) of *tawḥeed, "Lā ilāha ill-Allāh"* (لا إلـهَ إلا الله), came to correct belief – not only that of the ancient polytheists, but of all men up until the Day of Judgement. It testifies that there is no divinity except Allāh – none other than Him and none along with Him. None is similar to Him, none creates and sustains except Him, and none has the right to govern creation but Him. The concept of *tawḥeed* necessarily overflows into all aspects of belief and worship – into all aspects of life.

Whether he recognizes it or not, man is totally indebted to his Creator for his continuing existence hour by hour, not to mention such blessings as his many possessions and abilities. Knowing that Allāh alone is the Creator, the Sustainer, the Provider, the Controller, the source of all benefit and harm in whose hands is the Judgement and the final destination of men *requires* through common sense and reason that He alone be worshipped.

Although the concept of worship (*'ibādah*) has been gradually reduced in common usage to mean little more than the performance of certain religious rites and rituals, the original and true definition is comprehensive. It encompasses all actions and intentions motivated by a recognition of greatness – that combination of love and fear, producing efforts to please the worshipped one and to avoid his displeasure. An object of worship continually occupies the mind of the worshipper and consequently governs his behavior, both consciously and unconsciously. When applying the correct definition, it becomes clear that despite lip-service to *"Lā ilāha ill-Allāh,"* one's object of worship could well be something other than Allāh (*subḥānahu wa ta'ālā*).

﴿أَفَرَأَيْتَ مَنِ اتَّخَذَ إِلَـٰهَهُ هَوَاهُ وَأَضَلَّهُ اللهُ عَلَىٰ عِلْمٍ﴾

"Have you seen the one who takes as his god his own desire, and [so] Allāh has left him astray because of knowledge?" [178]

Those pursuers of falsehood in the form of political ideologies and national leaders, foreign customs, wealth, fashion or various worldly enjoyments might assume that by bowing to Allāh in prayer, they worship Him alone. But Prophet Muḥammad (ﷺ) firmly corrected this misconception. Once, 'Adiyy bin Ḥātim entered while the Prophet (ﷺ) was reciting a verse from the Qur'ān:

﴿اتَّخَذُوا أَحْبَارَهُمْ وَرُهْبَانَهُمْ أَرْبَابًا مِن دُونِ اللهِ وَالْمَسِيحَ ابْنَ مَرْيَمَ وَمَا أُمِرُوا إِلاَّ لِيَعْبُدُوا إِلَٰهًا وَاحِدًا﴾

"They took their scholars and monks as lords other than Allāh, and [also] the Messiah, Son of Mary. And they were not ordered except to worship one God..." [179] 'Adiyy (who had been a Christian), said, "O Messenger of Allāh, they did not worship them." The Prophet (ﷺ) replied, "Did they not tell them that the prohibited was lawful and that the lawful was prohibited and they followed them in that?" When 'Adiyy admitted, "Yes," the Prophet stated, "That was their worship of them."[180]

Thus worship was defined as obedience – a fact that becomes evident from even a superficial study of the Qur'ān, in which Allāh (*subḥānahu wa ta'ālā*) orders repeatedly:

﴿أَطِيعُوا اللهَ وَالرَّسُولَ﴾

---

[178] *Sūrah al-Jāthiyah,* 45:23. Scholars have said that the phrase "*'alā 'ilm*" ("*because of knowledge*") refers to Allāh's knowledge of that servant and his preference for his own desires, or as well, to that servant's knowledge of the truth although he rejects it.

[179] *Sūrah at-Tawbah,* 9:31.

[180] Aḥmad and at-Tirmidhī.

"Obey Allāh and the Messenger." [181]

﴿إِنِ الْحُكْمُ إِلَّا لِلَّهِ أَمَرَ أَلَّاتَعْبُدُوا إِلَّا إِيَّاهُ ذَلِكَ الدِّينُ الْقَيِّمُ وَلَكِنَّ أَكْثَرَ النَّاسِ لَايَعْلَمُونَ﴾

"Legislation is only for Allāh. He has commanded that you not worship any but Him. That is the right religion, but most of the people do not know." [182]

Two types of *shirk* were common both before and after the prophethood of Muḥammad (ﷺ). The first of these is the direction of acts of worship (especially supplication) to others besides Allāh while still claiming belief in Him. The Qur'ān orders:

﴿وَلَا تَدْعُ مَعَ اللهِ إِلَهًا آخَرَ لَا إِلَهَ إِلَّا هُوَ﴾

"And do not invoke besides Allāh another god. There is no god but Him." [183]

The other type of *shirk* is the willful adherence to laws and rulings other than His.

﴿أَلَمْ تَرَ إِلَى الَّذِينَ يَزْعُمُونَ أَنَّهُمْ آمَنُوا بِمَا أُنزِلَ إِلَيْكَ وَمَا أُنزِلَ مِن قَبْلِكَ يُرِيدُونَ أَن يَتَحَاكَمُوا إِلَى الطَّاغُوتِ وَقَدْ أُمِرُوا أَن يَكْفُرُوا بِهِ﴾

"Do you not consider those who claim to have believed in what was revealed to you and what was revealed before you? They wish to refer

---

[181] *Sūrahs* 3:32, 3:132, 4:59, 8:1, 8:20, 8:46, 24:54, 47:33, 58:13 and 64:12. Many other verses, although worded differently, carry the same meaning.

[182] *Sūrah Yūsuf,* 12:40.

[183] *Sūrah al-Qaṣaṣ,* 28:88.

legislation to ṭāghūt*[184] *while they were commanded to reject it."[185]

The loss of *tawḥeed* is sadly evident today in the acceptance of foreign philosophies and lifestyles, political oppression, innovations in religion, and countless forms of disobedience. Allāh (*subḥānahu wa ta'ālā*) warns:

﴿اتَّبِعُوا مَا أُنزِلَ إِلَيكُم مِن رَبِّكُم وَلاتَتَّبِعُوا مِن دُونِهِ أَولِيَاءَ﴾

"Follow what has been revealed to you from your Lord. And do not follow any patrons other than Him."[186]

﴿وَإِن تُطِع أَكثَرَ مَن فِي الأَرضِ يُضِلُّوكَ عَن سَبِيلِ اللهِ﴾

"And if you obey most of those upon the earth, they will lead you away from the path of Allāh."[187]

﴿وَإِنَّ كَثِيرًا لَّيُضِلُّونَ بِأَهوَائِهِم بِغَيرِ عِلمٍ﴾

"And certainly do many lead [others] astray through their own desires without knowledge."[188]

﴿وَلاتُطِع مَن أَغفَلنَا قَلبَهُ عَن ذِكرِنَا وَاتَّبَعَ هَوَاهُ وَكَانَ أَمرُهُ فُرُطًا﴾

"And do not obey one whose heart We have made unaware of Our remembrance and who

---

184 False objects of worship or those transgressors who usurp the divine right of government.

185 *Sūrah an-Nisā'*, 4:60.

186 *Sūrah al-A'rāf*, 7:3.

187 *Sūrah al-An'ām*, 6:116.

188 *Sūrah al-An'ām*, 6:119.

follows his desires and whose affair is excess [i.e., exceeding the limits of Allāh]."[189]

Reform will be accomplished only when the majority of Muslims has returned to the true worship of Allāh and will no longer tolerate *shirk.* The greater *jihād* against tyranny and oppression everywhere on earth will neither be accepted by Allāh nor aided by Him until the participants are truly dedicated to His cause and free of all other motivations. *Jihād* against the self and refinement of the soul are the first steps toward *jihād* for Islām.

﴿إِنَّ اللهَ لاَيُغَيِّرُ مَا بِقَوْمٍ حَتَّى يُغَيِّرُوا مَا بِأَنفُسِهِمْ﴾

"Indeed, Allāh will not change the condition of a people until they change what is in themselves..."[190]

The solution begins with the individual... in the soul.

---

[189] *Sūrah al-Kahf,* 18:28.
[190] *Sūrah ar-Ra'd,* 13:11.

REFERENCES

1. Al-Qur'ān ul-Kareem
2. *Ṣaḥeeḥ ul-Bukhārī* (*Fatḥ ul-Bārī bi Sharḥ Ṣaḥeeḥ il-Bukhārī*) by Ibn Ḥajar al-'Asqalānī
3. *Ṣaḥeeḥ Muslim* (*Mukhtaṣar Ṣaḥeeḥ Muslim*) (Beirut: al-Maktab ul-Islāmī)
4. *Majma'uz-Zawā'id wa Manba'ul Fawā'id* by al-Haythami (Cairo: Dār ar-Rayān)
5. *Riyādh uṣ-Ṣāliḥeen* by an-Nawawi (Beirut: Muassasat ur-Risālah)
6. *Majmū'u Fatāwā Shaykh il-Islām Aḥmad bin Taymiyyah* (Makkah: Ar-Ri'āsatul-'Aammah li Shu'ūn il-Ḥaramayn ish-Shareefayn)
7. *Fiqh us-Sunnah* by as-Sayyid Sābiq (Beirut: Dār ul-Kitāb il-'Arabi)
8. *Mukhtaṣar Minhāj il-Qāṣideen* by Aḥmad bin Qudāmah il-Maqdasi (Damascus: Maktabat Dār il-Bayān)
9. *Tahdheeb Madārij is-Sālikeen* by Ibn Qayyim il-Jawziyyah (Jeddah: Dār ul-Madanī)
10. *Al-Jawāb ul-Kāfi li Man Sa'ala 'an id-Dawā' ish-Shāfi* by Ibn Qayyim il-Jawziyyah
11. *Mafāheem Yanbaghi an Tuṣaḥḥaḥ* by Muḥammad Quṭb (Cairo: Dar ush-Shurūq)
12. *Aḥwāl ul-Ākhirati wa Ahwāluhā* by M. Salāmah Jabar (al-Kuwait: Dār ul-Istambūlī)